THE HERBARIUM OF FABRIC FLOWERS

Twenty Flower Brooch Projects Translated from Nature

UTOPIANO

SCHIFFER
PUBLISHING

4880 Lower Valley Road • Atglen, PA 19310

Introduction

I was once asked, "Flowers bloom every year, so why would you make them out of cloth?" Well, it is indeed said that live plants are the most precious. I agree; live plants are amazing and nothing can replicate them completely. But for example, if you are a painter, when you come across a beautiful landscape or an object that attracts you, you can't help but paint it. Even though deep down you know that your painting can never do justice to the real thing. I think making fabric flowers is the same sort of thing, and I just enjoy it so much.

What got me started was peering closely, very closely, at real plants, and then making my fabric flower patterns from them. At first, it was just plants and flowers I grew myself. Occasionally, I would use bouquets of flowers I received as a gift. In the future, if possible, I would like to visit the places where those flowers grow, and more specifically, I would like to observe them from germination until flowering. That's a goal of mine.

I have always been attracted by the beauty of plants in the north of Japan, so I began to visit the shores of Lake Toya in Hokkaido every year. I wondered if I could return there at different times of the year and observe the same plants over and over. How would their appearance change over time? And in a longterm relationship with them, I could take as much time as I needed to create my fabric flowers . . . These feelings have become even stronger since I rented a space for my studio in Shimarisuya, a small bakery by Lake Toya.

Recently, I wanted to make something resembling botanical specimens—just to look at. But many people told me that they would love to wear my fabric creations, like freshly picked flowers from a field. I am so very pleased to hear that and sentiments like that motivate me every day.

This book presents twenty different fabric flowers and the methods for making them. They range from simple fabric flower brooches—which I purposely designed so that even beginners can give it a try—to botanical specimen–like complex fabric flowers. The instructions reflect the methods I use to achieve my own particular vision. I think it's okay if you choose different steps to achieve your own results. As a matter of fact, the results should be different for everyone because we are all attracted to different aspects of any object, even if we are all looking at the same thing.

I truly hope that you too feel the pure joy of creating blooming flowers with your own hands!

utopiano

LXXI.e GENRE.

LE COLIOU, *COLIUS.*

Caractère général. Bec gros, convexe
en dessus, plus ou moins en dessous.

LE COLIOU.

IL nous paroit que le genre de cet oi-
seau doit être placé entre celui des
veuves et celui des bouvreuils; il tient
au premier par les deux longues plu-
mes qu'il a de même que les veuves au
milieu de la queue, et il s'approche du
second par la forme du bec, qui seroit
précisément la même que celle du bou-
vreuil, s'il étoit convexe en dessous
comme en dessus; mais il est applati

Jourdan Sculp.

1. LE COLIOU. 2. LE COLIOU DE L'ISLE DE PANAY.

Contents

COURS COMPLÉMENTAIRE DE LA LOUPE
HERBIER

à
Ordre
Couleur de Fleurs
Localité
Date de la récolte

COURS COMPLÉMENTAIRE DE LA LOUPE
HERBIER

à ....
Ordre
Couleur de Fleurs
Localité
Date de la récolte

5

Frilly Pansy

Scientific Name	*Viola × wittrockiana*
Scientific Classification	*Violaceae Viola*
Blooming Period	March through June

Instructions on p. 7

Until the beginning of the 19th century the pansy was a wildflower, and it was associated with large, colorful petals. However, developments in horticulture have advanced and improved since then, and while varieties that are similar to the wild pansy can still be found, more recently pansies have delicate colors and gentle ruffles. As our first project, here is a two-tone, chic brooch. Its petals are 2-ply and use glued cloth that has been dyed in gradated colors.

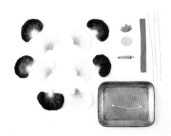

Materials

Stiffened cloth

Extra-fine cotton: Petal-a 4 pcs., Petal-b 4 pcs., Petal-c 2 pcs.
Thin crepe rayon: Calyx 1 pc., Stem cloth 90 x 10 mm / 3½" x ⅜"

Cotton satin: Brooch pin backing 1 pc.
Thin silk (*Usukinu*): Wire cloth

Pip
Mimosa pip 1 pc.

Jimaki wires
⅓ length green #26 1pc., ⅓ length #28 2 pcs.

Brooch pin
30 mm / 1¼" wide 1 pc.

COPIC Sketch Y17

Dyeing

Black Violet (Violet + Brown + Blue + Green)
Viola (Violet + Red Violet + Blue + Brown)
Leaf Green (Green + Brown + Sepia)
Gray Beige (Take some Viola on a brush and add it to pale Brown + Sepia + Green)

Petals: Dye in pairs. Dye uniformly with pale Gray Beige. Then, group the front side petals together and then also group the back side petals together. Gradate Viola on the base of the back side petals. While the front side petals are still damp, gradate Black Violet→Viola→Gray Beige inward from the edge. While still damp, once again add Black Violet inward from the edge and blend.

Calyx, Stem cloth: Dye Leaf Green.

Wire cloth: Uniformly dye a piece of thin silk with Leaf Green. Cut thin silk into 5 mm / ¼" wide strips (see p. 80).

Pip: Color with COPIC Sketch Y17.

1 Color pip head with the COPIC marker by tapping nib on pip head. Cut pip stem 20 mm / ¾" long as measured from below the colored pip head.

2 Apply glue to pip stem (from step 1) using a bamboo skewer. Attach three wires so pip stem is encased. This will create the flower stem. Cut to 90 mm / 3½" long.

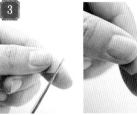

3 Cut end of wire cloth at an angle. Also, trim off about 2 mm / ¹⁄₁₆" from pointy end. Doing so will make binding easier.

4 Apply glue on wire cloth from step **3**. Align angled end with flower stem and bind once.

5 Keep trailing end of wire cloth taut and bind downward while applying glue little by little. This will prevent cloth from coming undone.

6 The cloth end is prone to unraveling. Apply glue generously and bind a little longer than flower stem. Press firmly on wire end with your fingers.

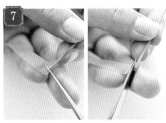

7 Conceal wire end with cloth and cut off any excess.

8 If cloth sticks out, apply glue and fold down.

9 Stretch stem cloth until it is about 95 mm / 3¾" long.

Apply glue to end of stem cloth and fold 1–2 mm / ¹⁄₁₆" inward. Press down. Do same for other end.

Before applying glue to the stem cloth, put the flower stem on the stem cloth and make sure that it doesn't protrude from both ends. Then apply the glue. Put the flower stem down so it is 1 mm / ¹⁄₁₆" in from the top edge.

Slowly roll cloth around the edge of flower stem. Once completely wrapped, if glue has dried up, just add more glue to tightly secure the seam.

Flower stem is complete.

Layer two pieces of cloth and cut out petals (see p. 79). Then, separate them into front side petal and back side petal. Dye accordingly.

Apply glue to inside of back side petal. Press down on a bamboo skewer and smear glue thinly and evenly all over.

Align petal bases and glue front and back together. It is okay if the edges are a bit misaligned. Please note this step cannot be undone and redone.

Note the slightly misaligned edge. Trim off excess petal cloth all the way around. Do not cut in small increments. Instead, try to cut in one smooth motion.

Add frills to edge before glue completely dries. Pinch edge with your fingers while slightly stretching up and down. Pinch four places for Petal-c, three places for both Petal-a and Petal-b.

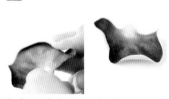

Curl curved edge inward with your fingers in a few places.

At 10 mm / ⅜" down from pip head, bend flower stem in a U-shape with pliers. Then, bend it another 10 mm / ⅜" down from the first bend. At this point, the stem cloth seam should be facing the back.

Apply glue to base of Petal-c.

Place pip head side on base of petal-c and tuck in.

Apply glue to pointy end of Petal-b's base.

With flower facing downward glue on each petal, all the while checking overall balance from front. Glue Petal-b on left side of Petal-c while aligning curve along base.

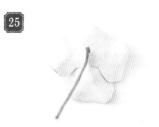

Next, apply glue to base of remaining b petals. Glue on right side of Petal-c, while aligning the base.

Next, apply glue to base of Petal-a and attach on top left corner of flower, while aligning the base.

Last, apply glue on base of remaining Petal-a piece and glue to the top right corner of the flower. Check overall balance from front.

Apply glue to backing cloth and attach to inside of brooch pin.

Attach brooch pin from step 28 above the flower stem on the back side of the flower. Leave pin undone until glue dries completely.

Apply glue to base of calyx.

Cover base of flower stem with calyx. Be sure to go around the flower stem. Use tweezers to adjust and add fine details.

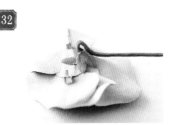

It looks like this from the side. The calyx center is aligned with the stem. It covers the base of the flower.

Our Frilly Pansy brooch is complete.

French Hydrangea

Scientific Name	*Hydrangea macrophylla*
Scientific Classification	*Hydrangeaceae Hydrangea*
Blooming Period	May through July

Instructions on p. 12

The French hydrangea is a flower whose colors change when they go unpruned in summer—or at least that is what I thought. In recent years, though, I've seen many French hydrangea varieties that have beautiful, deeply colored blooms even when pruned. Let's create French hydrangea blooms that resemble fluorite crystals, with their beautiful combinations of deep blue, azure, and grape. Many bunches of small florets are gathered together to make a large, ball-shaped flowerhead.

Materials

Stiffened cloth

Extra-fine cotton: Floret-a 9 pcs.
Cotton lawn: Floret-b 16 pcs.
Thin silk (*Usukinu*): Stem cloth

Pips

Small or ultra-small plain ball pip 25 pcs.

Jimaki wires

⅓ length green #22 1 pc., ½ length #30 6 pcs.

Brooch pin

30 cm / 11¾" wide 1 pc.

Brass soldering tip type

Triple Groove Chrysanthemum

Dyeing

Main Color (Turquoise + Green + Sepia)
Dull Green (Green + Turquoise + Brown + Sepia)
Grape (Violet + Red Violet + Brown)
Leaf Green (Olive Green + Sepia + Brown)
Gray Beige (Dip brush in Main Color and add to pale Brown + Sepia)

Floret: See p. 80. Dye in pairs. After dyeing very pale Gray Beige, drop in some of the Main Color to produce gradations. Add Dull Green and Grape to the edge and blend.

Stem cloth: Uniformly dye a piece of thin silk with Leaf Green. Cut thin silk into 5 mm / ¼" wide strips (see p. 80).

Shape the florets pieces. Shape each Floret-a separately. Shape Floret-b pieces in pairs. Firmly press the brass tip inward from the edge. Then, move the brass tip toward the center. After shaping each petal, turn over and press the brass tip into the center.

Pierce a hole at the center of the floret using an awl.

Cut off pip head on one end.

Bend edge of petal backward. If you have trouble doing this, moisten your fingertips with a wet towel and try again.

Insert pip in hole at center and apply glue both under the pip head and around the hole.

Push floret up until the base touches pip head. Pinch base of floret and tuck pip head inside.

While pinching pip head, twist one petal to create a nuanced look. It is not necessary to do this for every floret. Some of them can be plain.

After attaching a pip to all florets, mix Floret-a and Floret-b to make five floret bundles. For example, combining two Floret-a and three Floret-b, or combining one Floret-a and four Floret-b, etc.

Bind floret bundle stems from step 8 using #30 wire. Line up pip ends and align wire with middle.

While pressing down firmly with your thumbnail to prevent pip stems from shifting, wrap wire once and pull tightly. Repeat twice.

Hold wire firmly with your fingers, twist floret bundles a few turns to securely bind wire.

Fold wire from twist point and align with pips. Trim just the pips off at an angle.

Apply some glue on cut ends of pips. Bundle them together with wire.

To conceal where pips were bundled with wire, wrap 50 mm / 2" long (see p. 7) cloth around stem. Do the same for each bundle.

Make one bundle's stem straight. Bend two other bundle stems a little below wire. Bend remaining bundle's stem a little bit deeper than the other two bundles.

Sandwich straight stem bundle between slightly bent bundles.

Add other two bundles—with more angled stems—in front of bundles from step **16**.

When viewed from behind, the three bundles from step **16** should line up flat. Making the back side flat helps when attaching brooch pin.

Use #30 wire to bind all five bundles together. Similar to step **9**, after binding twice, twist to secure. This time twist on the side, not at the front or back.

Lift wire on back side with tweezers.

Apply glue to tip of #22 wire and insert in gap created in previous step. Return lifted wire to its original position.

13

Cut bundled stems at 25–30 mm / 1"–1¼" and start wrapping stem cloth from wire location. Wrap stem cloth a little longer than stem ends. Press end with fingernails and fold stem cloth.

Apply glue to bottom of flower stem and then cover end with stem cloth. Fold cloth upward.

Flip upside down, apply glue to end of stem cloth and wrap flower stem around once. Cut excess at back.

Attach brooch pin to the back. Apply glue on stem cloth and wrap flower stem twice just below wire.

Lay brooch pin on back side of flower stem.

Apply glue to stem cloth and wrap brooch pin once. Hold stem cloth taut and wait a little. Repeat this four or five times to bind brooch pin to flower stem.

Leave pin undone until glue has completely dried.

The French Hydrangea brooch is complete.

Round Leaf Eucalyptus

Scientific Name	*Eucalyptus*
Scientific Classification	*Myrtaceae Eucalyptus*
Blooming Period	February through May

Instructions on p. 82

There are hundreds of eucalyptus varieties. Their leaves come in many shapes and sizes: *Eucalyptus polyanthemos*, *Eucalyptus gunnii*, *Corymbia citriodora*, and others. Some of these varieties are increasingly seen in gardens in residential areas. The pattern for this particular brooch is made from a branch of *Eucalyptus gunnii*. The real leaves are flat, but the leaves of this brooch were rounded a bit to produce a more nuanced look.

16

Eucalyptus with Buds

Scientific Name	*Eucalyptus*
Scientific Classification	*Myrtaceae Eucalyptus*
Blooming Period	May through July

Instructions on p. 18

This eucalyptus twig has buds. The pattern was made from the branch of *Eucalyptus polyanthemos* whose heart-shaped leaves grew into a teardrop shape. When dried, the foliage of *Eucalyptus polyanthemos* transforms into a beautiful silvery color. When *Eucalyptus polyanthemos* blooms, the pointy hat-like parts of its buds come off, thus revealing pretty flowers spreading radially from the pistils.

Instructions: Eucalyptus with Buds

Full size pattern: p. 83

Materials

Stiffened cloth
Extra-fine cotton: Leaf-A 2 pcs., Leaf-B 2 pcs.
Thin silk (*Usukinu*): Buds, Stem cloth

Pip
Small ball pip 16 pcs.

Jimaki wires
½ length green #26 3 pcs., ⅓ length green #26 1 pc., ½ length #28 2 pcs., ½ length #30 1 pc.

Brooch pin
25 mm / 1" wide 1 pc.

Brass soldering tip type
Ultra-thin Single Groove Chrysanthemum

Dyeing

Silver Green (Olive Green + Turquoise + Brown + Sepia)
Accent Color (Dip a brush in Silver Green and add it to Brown + Sepia)
Base Color (pale Accent Color)

Leaf: After dyeing the Base Color, add Silver Green while the cloth is still damp. Drop in the Accent Color on the base and blend.

Buds, Stem cloth: Uniformly dye a piece of thin silk Silver Green. Cut thin silk into 10 x 10 mm / ⅜" x ⅜" squares for buds, and into 5 mm / ¼" wide strips for stems (see p. 80).

Pip: Dye a green that is close to leaf color.

1

Make buds. Cut thin silk cloth into sixteen 10 x 10 mm / ⅜" x ⅜" square pieces according to pip head size. Pierce hole at center of each square using an awl.

2

Cut pip head on one end at an angle. Insert pip into hole pierced in step **1** and apply glue on square cloth.

3

Cover pip head and pinch and twist cloth to make pointy. Do the same for sixteen buds.

4

Bind buds. Apply glue on tip of #26 wire and attach three buds. Bind wire and pip stem with stem cloth for about 15 mm / ⅝". Do not cut off stem cloth yet.

5

Without a wire, bind two buds together with another stem cloth for about 10 mm / ⅜". In a similar manner, make a bundle of three buds.

6

Also, make a bundle of five buds with #30 wire. Bind wire and pip stem with stem cloth for about 20 mm / ¾".

7

Cut off pip stems on bundle from step **4** at an angle (do not cut wire). Then, add two bundles of buds from step **5**. Bind together with stem cloth for 10 mm / ⅜".

8

Add bundle of three buds from step **5**. Bind together for another 10 mm / ⅜" with stem cloth.

9

Combine bundle of five buds from step **6**. Bind together for another 20 mm / ¾" with stem cloth. This bundle of buds is going to be paired with Leaf-A.

10 Make another bundle of three buds with ⅓ length #26 wire. Bind together with stem cloth for 20 mm / ¾". This bundle of buds is going to be paired with Leaf-B.

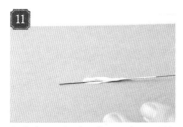

11 Make leaves. Apply soft-type glue on #28 wire. Put some glue on a piece of paper and coat wire while turning. Coat evenly and thinly.

12 Smear a thin layer of soft-type glue on inside of leaf cloth. Place wire from step **11** lengthwise at 5 mm / ¼" down from leaf tip.

13 Put paired leaf cloth on top and glue pair together. Trim off about 1–2 mm / 1/16" from edge once glue has dried.

14 Shape leaves. Use Ultra-thin Single Groove Chrysanthemum brass tip. From base of leaf, trace along wire all the way to leaf tip.

15 Twist cloth with your fingers in two places based on the curves produced by hot-pressing to produce a nuanced look.

16 These two leaves are complete.

17 Apply glue to #26 wire tip and attach to leaf base. Bind them with stem cloth for 30 mm / 1¼". Do not cut stem cloth! Leave as is.

18 Combine Leaf-A and bud bundle from step **9**. Combine Leaf-B and bud bundle from step **10**. Apply glue to stem cloth and bind each set of leaves and buds twice. Cut stem cloth on Leaf-B bundle.

19 Now, combine Leaf-A branch and Leaf-B branch. Bind them together with Leaf-A branch stem cloth. Wrap stem cloth for about 30 mm / 1¼". Cut off excess wire. Treat wire end as on p. 14.

20 Attach brooch pin. After wrapping stem cloth a few times around the back side of the stem, place brooch pin on stem. Refer to p. 14 and attach brooch pin so that leaves face downward when worn.

21 Your Eucalyptus with Buds brooch is complete.

Persian Buttercup

Scientific Name	*Ranunculus asiaticus*
Scientific Classification	*Ranunculales Ranunculus*
Blooming Period	March through May

Instructions on p. 22

Ranunculus flowers come in a variety of shapes and colors, from multi-layered gorgeous blooms to lustrous single layer blooms. I made the pattern for this particular work from Ranunculus 'Reinette Orange,' whose stamens look like leaves. I tried to capture the fully bloomed look for this brooch.

Full size pattern: p. 108

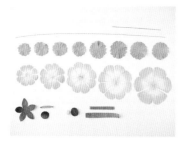

Materials

Stiffened cloth

Thin silk (*Usukinu*): Corolla-a 4 pcs., -b 4 pcs., -c 4 pcs., -d 4 pcs., and -e 2 pcs., Wire cloth Cotton lawn: Stamen-A 1 pc., Stamen-B 3 pcs., Stamen-C 4 pcs.

Super-fine velvet: Calyx 1 pc., Pistil 1 pc., Stem cloth 12 x 80 mm / ½" x 3⅛", Brooch pin backing 1 pc.

Styrene ball

Mini-rose flower core 8 mm / ¼" width 1 pc.

Jimaki wires

⅓ length green #26 1 pc., #30 1 pc.

Brooch pin

30 cm / 11¾" wide 1 pc.

Brass soldering tip type

Forget-me-not, Single Groove Chrysanthemum

Dyeing

Yellow Brown (Yellow + Sepia + Brown)
Base (pale Sepia)
Leaf Green (Olive Green + Sepia + Brown)

Corolla: Dye a layer of four corolla cloths all at once (dye the Corolla-e cloths in two piece layers). Uniformly dye the corolla cloths in Base Color. While still damp, gradate Yellow Brown from the edge to the center. Drop pale Leaf Green at center.

Stamen, Pistil, Calyx, Brooch pin backing, Stem cloth: Dye Leaf Green.

Wire cloth: Uniformly dye a piece of thin silk in Leaf Green. Cut thin silk into 5 mm / ¼" wide strips (see p. 80).

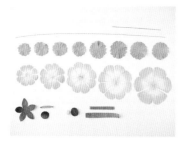

Use an awl to pierce a hole, widthwise, in the styrene ball. It should be slightly below center.

Thread #30 wire through hole and twist at bottom of styrene ball.

Press Forget-me-not brass tip at center of pistil cloth on the back side.

Apply glue to styrene ball from step **2** and cover pistil cloth.

Add #26 wire while aligning with pistil stem. Cut wire to 75 mm / 3" long. Bind wire and pistil stem using wire cloth (see page 7).

Pierce hole at center of corolla cloth and press Forget-me-not brass tip on two layer corolla cloth. Drag brass tip from edge to center on a soft ironing sponge.

Shape stamen cloth pieces. Slide Single Groove Chrysanthemum brass tip from edge to center. Pierce hole at center using an awl.

Shape calyx cloth. Pierce hole at center with an awl. Slide Single Groove Chrysanthemum brass tip from each pointy tip to the center.

Insert pistil stem through Stamen-A cloth. Then, apply glue to bottom of styrene ball and Stamen-A cloth, moving out from center to just a little above the notches.

10

Turn upside down and wrap your fingers around Stamen-A cloth to glue it on pistil.

11

Looking down from above, adjust edges of Stamen-A so they are angled inward.

12

Similarly, glue three Stamen-B cloth pieces on, one-by-one, then four Stamen-C pieces. Make the stamens look like they are gradually opening.

13

Apply glue to back side of stamen cloth.

14

Begin to glue corolla cloths on, one-by-one, beginning from Corolla-a. Glue on by spreading center of each corolla flat.

15

Glue on corolla cloth while shifting the positioning of the petals to be separate from the corolla underneath. Do the same for remaining Corolla-a pieces.

16

After gluing on four corolla cloths of the same size, make a circle with your fingers. Wrap flower around to adjust shape.

17

Next, begin to glue on four cloths of both Corolla-b, -c and -d. Adjust bloom shape after gluing every fourth corolla cloth.

18

All corolla cloths, including two Corolla-e, are glued on.

19

Place bamboo skewer lengthwise on back side of stem cloth. Pinch stem cloth lightly to curl. This will help wrap the stem.

20

Apply glue on right side of the stem cloth lengthwise. Then, lay stem on glue. Fold down right side of stem cloth, where glue was applied.

21

Trim off stem cloth 2 mm / $\frac{1}{16}$" below stem.

Apply glue on remaining half of stem cloth. Then, fold down to wrap stem completely.

The stem end is hollow for 2 mm / ¹⁄₁₆".

Attach calyx cloth. Make an incision from notch to center.

Make a small incision along the hot-pressed line on each sepal.

Apply glue a little above calyx cloth notches.

Position stem cloth seam facing away from you. Calyx incision should be in front of you. Then, cover flower base with calyx cloth. Do not overlap detached sides, instead butt them up to each other.

Tilt flower by bending stem at calyx base. Then, attach brooch pin in same manner as p. 9. Attach backing cloth so that it grips the stem.

Curve the stem as desired. While holding the center of the bloom, curve the wire little by little.

Back side view.

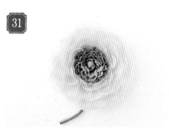

Our Persian Buttercup brooch is complete.

Poppy Anemone

Scientific Name	*Anemone coronaria*
Scientific Classification	*Ranunculaceae Anemone*
Blooming Period	April through May

Instructions on p. 28

In Greek, *anemone* means "Daughter of the Wind." What looks like petals are actually sepals. This is the result of a calyx mutation, and these plant sections are called tepals. The leaf-like thing just below its flower is the calyx. Since the wire of each sepal is bound together with the flower stem, the angle of each tepal can be manipulated to create a closed or open bloom. Attaching the tepals in a way that makes the bloom look open shows the stamen crowns and creates a wonderful look.

Materials

Stiffened cloth

Extra-fine cotton: Tepal-A 2 pcs., Tepal-B 10 pcs., Tepal-C 8 pcs.

Thin silk (*Usukinu*): Wire cloth

Super-fine velvet: Calyx 1 pc., Pistil 1 pc., Stem cloth 12 x 80 mm / ½" x 3⅛" and 15 x 20 mm / ⅝" x ¾"

Styrene ball

8 mm / ¼" diameter 1 pc.

Pips

Rose or plain ball black pip 30 pcs.

Jimaki wires

⅓ length green #26 1pc., #30 1 pc., ⅓ length #30 10 pcs.

Brooch pin

30 mm / 1¼" wide 1 pc.

Brass soldering tip types

9 mm / ⅜" Hemisphere, 15 mm / ⅝" Hemisphere, Ultra-thin Single Groove

Dyeing

Red (Red + Sepia + Scarlet)
Base Color (Sepia)
Leaf Green (Olive Green + Sepia + Brown)

Tepal: Dye pale Base Color. While still damp, dye tepal cloth edges Red. Gradate at base. Dye back side same as front.
Pistil: Dye Red. Then, drop in Leaf Green while cloth is still damp to produce blackish red color.
Calyx, Stem cloth: Dye Leaf Green.
Wire cloth: Uniformly dye a piece of thin silk Leaf Green. Cut thin silk into 5 mm / ¼" wide strips (see p. 80).

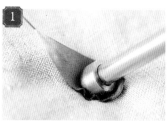

1 Put ⅓ length #30 wire, 15–20 mm / ⅝"–¾" tip from wire end, between base of a pair of tepal cloth pieces. Glue together. Trim off misaligned edge. Shape tepal piece on soft sponge using soldering iron.

2 Use 9 mm / ⅜" Hemisphere brass tip for Tepal-A and 15 mm / ⅝" Hemisphere brass tip for Tepal-B. Face the wire away from you, on a soft sponge and hot-press from inside edge to base of tepal. Press down on the brass tip at widest point.

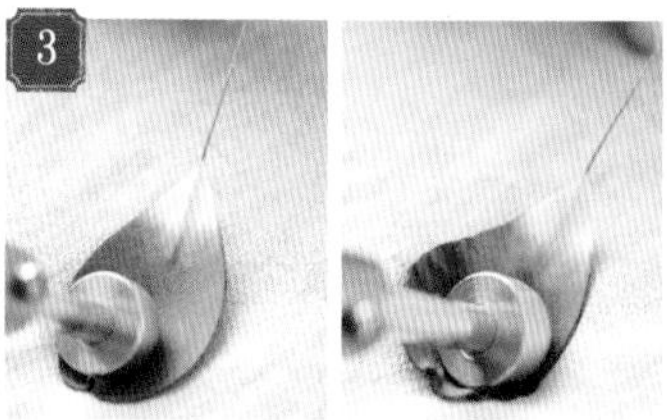

3 Use 15 mm / ⅝" Hemisphere brass tip for Tepal-C. Press brass tip down just inside the edge and move towards base. Do this for left and right edges separately. Then, press brass tip from center to base of tepal. Push down brass tip at widest point.

4 Place pistil cloth on soft sponge and push down with 9 mm / ⅜" Hemisphere brass tip.

5 Shape calyx cloth. Press down Ultra-thin Single Groove brass tip on the back side. Press from outside to center.

6 On the front side, press brass tip at base to create three lines.

7 Pierce center of styrene ball with an awl. Then, put #30 wire through the hole and twist wire at the bottom of the ball (see p. 22). Insert ⅓ length of #26 wire.

8 Bind wires together with wire cloth under styrene ball.

9 Apply glue to styrene ball and pistil cloth. Cover ball with pistil cloth from step **4**.

10

Bind and glue ten pips. Cut pip stems to 15 mm / ⅝". Hold base of bundle and spread pip heads to make a fan-shape (see p. 50). Make six bundles. Glue each bundle around base of pistil.

11

Bend wire 2–3 mm / ¹⁄₁₆" above base of each tepal.

12

Apply glue on base of tepal and attach to base of pistil and stamen from step **10**. Begin attaching Tepal-A pieces.

13

Glue on three Tepal-B pieces, one-by-one, without overlapping. At the end, glue on one Tepal-B piece that slightly overlaps the Tepal-A.

14

Glue on remaining Tepal-B piece between -A and -B on the stem. Glue on four Tepal-C pieces, one-by-one, to fill gaps. Check overall balance and adjust height of each tepal so there won't be any space between the pieces.

15

Close bloom to make wrapping stem cloth easier. Trim off stem at 75 mm / 3" from base and bind with wire cloth.

16

Refer to p. 8 and close stem cloth.

17

Press thumbnail against base of flower to bend stem. Before you bend, make sure stem cloth seam is toward the back.

18

Attach brooch pin to base on back side. Apply glue to wire cloth and wrap around stem a few times. Bind brooch pin to stem.

19

Apply glue to stem cloth (15 x 20 mm / ⅝" x ¾"). Start to cover wire cloth that binds brooch pin to stem beginning from one corner. Butt head and tail of stem cloth together and cut off excess.

20

Curve stem a little and glue on calyx cloth. Apply glue on front side at base of calyx. Attach below stem cloth that binds brooch pin, facing slightly to the right. Pull down each segment of the calyx to expose right side.

21

Open bloom and position pistil at center. The Poppy Anemone brooch is complete.

Christmas Rose

Scientific Name	*Helleborus niger*
Scientific Classification	*Ranunculaceae Helleborus*
Blooming Period	December through April

Instructions on p. 32

Christmas roses with simple rounded petals look nice. Other types have gorgeous, layered petals that also look fantastic. Christmas rose flowers give off a serene impression because of their simple appearance and the way the flowers tilt downward. It also has tepals, meaning mutated sepals. The actual petals have degenerated into nectar glands that remain around the stamens. The bracts that are attached as if they were protecting the flowers are very attractive as the flower color is faintly cast down on them.

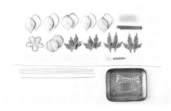

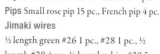

Styrene ball 10 mm / ⅜" diameter 1 pc.
Pips Small rose pip 15 pc., French pip 4 pc.
Jimaki wires
½ length green #26 1 pc., #28 1 pc., ½
length #28 4 pc., ½ length white #30 5 pc.
Brooch pin 30 mm / 1¼" wide 1 pc.
Brass soldering tip type
21 mm / ¾" Hemisphere, Large Petal, Ultra-thin Petal, Ultra-thin Single Groove

Materials

Stiffened cloth

Pure silk satin crepe #10: Tepal-A 6 pcs.,
Tepal-B 4 pcs.
Pure silk satin crepe #14: Bud 1 pc.
Cotton lawn: Nectary 2 pcs., Bract-A 4 pcs.,
Bract-B 4 pcs.
Thin silk (*Usukinu*): Pistil 30 x 30 mm /
1¼" x 1¼" 2 pcs. Stem cloth

Dyeing

Base Color (Dip a brush in Leaf Green and
add to Brown + Sepia)
Red Violet (Red Violet + Red + Brown +
Green)
Leaf Green (Green + Sepia + Brown)
Yellow Grown (Yellow + Brown)

Tepal, Nectary, Bud: Dye the tepal cloth
in pairs. Dye the bud and nectary cloth one
piece at a time. Use a very pale Base Color
to dye each cloth uniformly. Gradate Leaf
Green at the base and center of each cloth.
Once excess moisture has evaporated, add
Red Violet along the edge and soften with
the pale Base Color. Once completely dry,
add a fine line of Red Violet along the edge.
Pips: Dye the rose pips Yellow Brown. As for
the French pips, use commercially available
yellow-green colored pips.
Pistil, Stem cloth: Uniformly dye a piece of
thin silk Leaf Green. Cut thin silk into 5 mm
/ ¼" wide strips (see p. 80).
Bract: After uniformly dye Leaf Green, add
pale Red Violet at tip of each segment on
bract cloth.

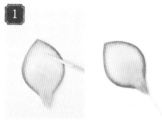

1. Lightly apply hard-type glue, in dots, on
tepal cloth. Sandwich a #30 white wire
between a pair tepal cloths, at the base.
Glue them together.

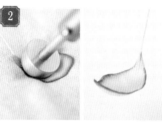

2. Put tepal piece on a soft sponge. Press a
21 mm / ¾" Hemisphere brass tip down
on base of tepal. Be as careful as possible
not to wrinkle or tuck the cloth.

3. Bend wire at 5 mm / ¼" above base of
tepal.

4. Insert #28 wire between two pieces of bract
cloth and glue together. Trim off misaligned
edges. On a hard sponge, press Ultra-thin
Single Groove brass tip down on back side of
bract. Move the brass tip from outside of each
bract segment toward center.

5. Turn bract piece right-side up. For each
segment, press Ultra-thin Single Groove
brass tip toward center on base of bract.
Bend wire at base of bract.

6. Glue two pieces of thin silk together.
After the glue has dried, cut out three
pieces of pistil pieces (see photo). Bias
cut thin silk to 20–25 mm / ¾"–1" long.
Taper ends.

7. Hot-press Ultra-thin Single Groove brass
tip on a hard sponge.

8. Glue pistil strips from step **7** around the
½ length #26 wire (see photo). Bind stem
cloth around wire.

9. In the same manner as on p. 50, glue
together stems of five bundled rose
pips. Cut stem to 15 mm / ⅝". Make six
bundles. Glue on these bundles, encasing
pistils glued on the wire in step **8**.

10

Cut the stem of each French pip to 20 mm / ¾". Glue French pip, one piece at a time, around stem from step **9**. Bind stem cloth around once.

11

Shape nectary cloth using Ultra-thin Petal brass tip. Hot-press each cloth separately and move brass tip from the tip of each segment to the center.

12

Apply glue on base of nectary cloth. Pinch with your fingers and fold base of nectary in half. At center of folded part, make cuts in the shape of an asterisk. Repeat process for the other nectary piece.

13

Coat stem cloth with glue from step **10**. Thread each nectary cloth through the wire and attach separately.

14

Begin to attach tepals. Apply glue on the wire and base of Tepal-A. Glue it under nectary. Attach second Tepal-A on the right, slightly overlapping first Tepal-A. Attach third Tepal-A on opposite side.

15

Attach one Tepal-B between the first and third Tepal-A. Attach remaining Tepal-B between second and third Tepal-A, as if covering it from the outside (do not overlap inside). Proceed to making the bud.

16

Press Large Petal brass tip on outside of each segment of bud cloth. Move toward center. Perforate center with awl. Thread #28 wire through styrene ball (see p. 22) and bind the wire with stem cloth at base of ball.

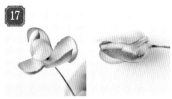

17

Apply glue to styrene ball and thread bud cloth through the wire. Cover ball with one segment of bud cloth. Then, attach segment to right. Next, attach the segment opposite from the first and second segments. Apply glue on base of remaining segment of bud cloth. Gently cover of ball from outside.

18

Bind stem cloth around wire a few times and apply glue to base of Bract-A pieces. Attach on each side of bud. Bind wires with stem cloth for about 60 mm / 2⅜". Dispose of stem cloth at wire end (see p. 14). Angle the bud downward.

19

Combine flower with Bract-B pieces and bind them with stem cloth for 70 mm / 2 ¾" in a similar manner to the bud. Same as step **18**, angle flower downward at bract base. Cover flower with bracts and adjust overall shape.

20

Combine flower and bud while aligning where wire is bent. Bind them with stem cloth a few times. Attach brooch pin (see p. 14).

21

The Christmas Rose brooch is complete.

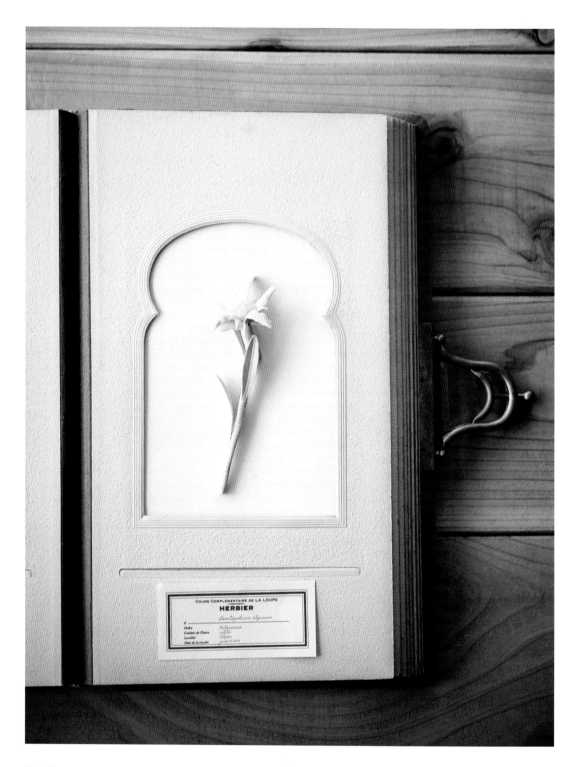

The image shows a black-and-white photograph of an open herbarium book resting on a wooden surface. A pressed edelweiss flower is displayed within an arched cutout window in the page. A label at the bottom reads:

COURS COMPLÉMENTAIRE DE LA LOUPE
HERBIER
Leontopodium alpinum
Ordre *Asteraceae*
Couleur de Fleurs *white*
Localité *Alpine*
Date de la récolte *June, 2016*

Edelweiss

Scientific Name	*Leontopodium nivale*
Scientific Classification	*Asteraceae Leontopodium*
Blooming Period	July through September

Instructions on p. 84

The star-like white petals are actually the bracts, which are essentially deformed leaves. Edelweiss has a small yellow dot-like flower at the center. Edelweiss is very resistant to cold, and dense hair covers the plant in order to protect it from aridity and strong sunlight. Velvet is used here to represent the dense hair and thickness of Edelweiss. A thin layer of cotton fibers covers the center of the flower.

White Clover

Scientific Name	*Trifolium repens*
Scientific Classification	*Fabaceae Trifolium*
Blooming Period	April through December

Instructions on p. 86

The Japanese name for white clover, *shirotsume kusa* ("white stuffing grass"), comes from the fact that, during the Edo period (1603-1868), dried white clover was stuffed in gaps around glassware being shipped in from the Netherlands to prevent breakage. Sometimes I have a vision in which white clover is guarding something fragile, but quite important, under its leaves. Something like a bird's egg. Ever since I was a child, wildflowers have been in my general orbit and I have always felt that they were gentle. They make me kind of nostalgic. This brooch can be worn as if it were just picked from a field! It has such a subtle and casual feel.

White Clover

After a decade working in the world of arts and crafts, I took up a completely different profession. At that point in my life, posting photos on Instagram of the roses and violets I grew was a great pleasure. It was a small means of expressing who I was. Back then, I thought I would never return to my previous profession. Honestly, when I first started on Instagram, I met a bunch of people and we became friends after exchanging emails. I still stay in touch with them.

In retrospect, I think the silk flowers that I made for those friends whom I had not yet met in person formed the origins of my current production style. To celebrate the birthday of one of these friends, I picked white clover to make a silk flower. While I was observing that little white clover I became inspired to make something more simple and elegant, instead of just something girlish or cute. This silk flower, a gift to my friend—which I had actually drawn from the real plant—was the impetus for me to be accepted as an artist back into the world of arts and crafts.

I intended to send the silk flower with a box full of dried white clover, to replicate its use as cushioning material in the past. So, I went to a store in Kamakura to search for a box. Mrs. Fukuyama, the owner of Patrone—the store I went to—was interested in the white clover brooch I brought to size up the box. I remember how happy I was when she showed interest in the actual silk flower I had produced, not a digital image on a computer or cell phone screen.

At first, the shop sold my white clover brooches and Christmas rose corsages. Since my works were sold at a physical retail store—rather than virtually—I was offered a few exhibitions. Also, I was able to hold workshops on a regular basis at the store because of my previous experience as an instructor.

Naoko Tachiko is a friend to whom I presented a white clover brooch. She is a designer at Fridge Inc., and I asked her to design utopiano's logo, business cards, and paper boxes when I started my career as a silk flower artist. For me, white clover is a plant that has brought many opportunities and good fortune.

In a tin box filled with white clover silk flowers, I put two white clover brooches for my friend Naoko and her daughter. In order to subtly hide the brooch pins under the base of the flower and allow the brooches to blend in naturally with the other white clover in the box, I came up with the shape of a leaf's stem wrapped around the flower's stem in an S-shape. There was a reason behind this form. In reality, white clover stems don't actually wrap like that. But it mirrors the original "White Clover Brooch" first sold at the Patrone store.

Sweet Violet

Scientific Name	*Viola odorata*
Scientific Classification	*Violaceae Viola*
Blooming Period	December through March

Instructions on p. 88

What is your favorite scent? If I were to be asked that question, I probably wouldn't hesitate to say sweet violet. It has such a powdery sweet scent and lovely appearance. The heart-shaped leaves and downward looking blooms, the stria that serve as runways for insects to stop and suck the nectar that accumulates in the spur . . . it's all so wonderful. Let's make a fabric flower version of sweet violet while carefully examining each of its elements.

Sweet Violet

> Do you think amethysts can be the souls of good violets?
> —L.M. Montgomery, *Anne of Green Gables*

Just as Anne had her "Violet Vale," I had my "Valley of Violets" when I was a child. It was a secret place where many sweet violets would bloom in the spring, and I used to daydream that there were sparkling minerals buried under the roots of those violets. The "Violets and Minerals" exhibition that I held a few years ago with Kobutsu Asobi—who promotes the beauty of minerals on social media—was an exhibition rooted in that childhood fantasy.

The violet I grew was mostly sweet violet, but I also love Viola Sororia, or 'Freckles.' It has freckles on its narrow, graceful blue violet petals. At one time, I was even a member of the Japan Violet Society. Just looking through the pamphlets listing violet seed varieties sent to me once a year was fun. My mind was filled with fantasies of beautiful violet flowers. However, I didn't have much success growing violets from seeds. So now I grow them by acquiring violet seedlings that glow along the soil surface.

The theme of my first solo exhibition, "utopiano," was also sweet violet. When dividing the plant, I really loved the look of roots hanging down from the sweet violet. So, I made fabric

sweet violet with roots. Back then, I don't think I ever saw any fabric flowers with roots. Someone once told me that there shouldn't be brown roots on items that you wear. So, to represent the roots, I would just wrap green stem cloth around the area where the roots should be. In recent years, I've been told the opposite quite a few times—that with botanical specimens, fabric flower brooches *should* have brown roots. I find this quite interesting.

And strangely enough, when I held the violet themed exhibition, sometimes people who loved violets would quietly tell me their violet stories. The appearance of small violets, with their downward pointing blooms, and their scent may have hidden powers that make people *want* to discuss their nostalgic memories.

Scent and Flavor of Violet

I have a weakness for violet flavored food, and whenever I find imported violet flavored candies or liqueurs, it's very hard to resist. In Europe, they use sweet violet to flavor foods. They even use it as an herb in salads and pasta! Every year, I make a syrup from sweet violet. And even though I can only make a little bit, I think it's like food for the soul . . .

European Mistletoe

Scientific Name	*Viscum album*
Scientific Classification	*Santalaceae Viscum*
Blooming Period	February through April

Instructions on p. 90

After the leaves of deciduous trees fall, you may notice something like a bird's nest or a paper lantern on the branches of the trees. European mistletoe, with its leaves that stay green, even in winter, was believed to have sacred powers. Passing under European mistletoe is thought to be good luck. It was thought that hanging mistletoe on the front door at Christmas would ward off evil. The white berries of the European mistletoe, the honey-colored berries found in Japan, and the tomatillo-like red berries are expressed using natural stones and glass beads.

European Mistletoe

The birch tree and shiny clouds evaporating
Over there, golden berries of the European Mistletoe
Glow quietly
—Excerpt from "Winter and Galaxy Station" in *An Asura in Spring*, Kenji Miyazawa

When was the last time you actually saw European mistletoe that appears Kenji Miyazawa's poetry or in children's literature? My first time seeing European mistletoe, it had white berries and was drawn on an antique European greeting card. I was told that this color is not found in Japan. The European mistletoe I saw on my trip was very high up on the tree, and it had tomatillo colored berries. I really wanted to see those golden colored berries up close someday.

I'll never forget the first time they actually had European mistletoe at a local flower shop. It had smooth green branches and translucent, honey-colored berries. After that, every year in December, I would think about European mistletoe and wait anxiously for it to arrive. When I posted a photo of it on Instagram, people often asked me, "What is that plant?" In the past few years, more and more florists have been working with mistletoe, and I've been seeing more and more of it in town. It's a pleasant surprise.

European mistletoe is a parasitic plant that lives on a host. On massive trees, some of which are over three hundred years old, the mistletoe may cause the tree to weaken. I've found an organization that harvests European mistletoe in the presence of a tree doctor for the purpose of ensuring the well-being of the tree. And I now get European mistletoe through that organization. It doesn't just deliver European mistletoe to me, it also reports on what kind of tree it was living on, its location, and how the harvesting went. Given that I always wanted to know as much as possible about the plant and where it grows, I am very pleased with the fact that they tell me everything about the mistletoe.

When the air is cool and crisp, I trace the mistletoe shapes that have made their way to me from high up in the trees. I hang it by the window and I sketch the branches and berries that have fallen from the mistletoe knots. It is all for next year, just so that I can replicate this lovely European mistletoe with cloth.

Since I started making fabric flowers, I have thankfully been given the opportunity to exhibit my work. My fabric flowers have taken me many places. And wherever I go, I look for European mistletoe and go to the locales where it grows.

The only wish I ever make under the mistletoe is that I can come back to see it again.

COURS COMPLÉMENTAIRE DE LA LOUPE
HERBIER

à _____ *Rosa rugosa*
Ordre *Rosa rosa*
Couleur de Fleurs *Rose*
Localité *Japan*
Date de la récolte *June 20 2016*

Ramanas Rose

Scientific Name	*Rosa rugosa*
Scientific Classification	*Rosaceae Rosa*
Blooming Period	May through August

Instructions on p. 50

This is a strongly scented rose found mainly in the sandy soil of the Hokkaido coast. The leaves have fine crepe-like wrinkles on their surface. Ramanas rose may have white colored blooms, but that's very rare. A hybrid of Ramanas rose and Baby rose (*Rosa multiflora*) has small-sized pink colored blooms. In the Toya area of Hokkaido, you can see both white flowering Ramanas rose and the pink hybrid. I made the pattern for this brooch from one I collected lakeside in Toya.

Materials

Stiffened cloth

Extra-fine cotton: Petal-a 6 pcs., Petal-b 4 pcs.

Thin crepe rayon: Leaf-A 2 pcs., Leaf-B 8 pcs., Leaf-C 2 pcs., Stipule 1 pc., Calyx 1 pc.

Thin silk (*Usukinu*): Stem cloth

Pips

Small or ultra-small rose pip 25 pcs.

Jimaki wires

⅓ length green #26 1 pc., ½ length #28 2 pcs., #30 1 pc., ½ length #30 4 pcs.

Brooch pin

30 mm / 1¼" wide 1 pc.

Cotton

Brass soldering tip type

Ultra-thin Single Groove

Dyeing

Rose Red (Rhodamine Red + Red + Brown)

Beige (Brown + Sepia)

Leaf Green (Green + Sepia + Brown)

Petals: Dye in pairs. Uniformly dye pale Beige. While still damp, dye edge with Rose Red and gradate towards base. Flip and dye back side the same as the front. Gradate Beige again from base.

Leaf, Stipule, Calyx: Dye uniformly Leaf Green.

Stem cloth: Uniformly dye a piece of thin silk Leaf Green. Cut thin silk into 5 mm / ¼" wide strips (see p. 80).

Pip: Dye yellow color.

1 Make pistil. Cut five pips in half, but then bundle a total of ten together while aligning heads. Wrap #30 wire around twice and put loose wire ends over pip heads (see photo). Then, bundle together. Bind with stem cloth once.

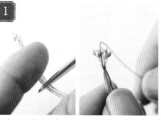

2 Make stamens. Bundle five pips and apply glue 10 mm / ⅜" below heads. Pinch pip stems together to bind. Cut pip stems at 15 mm / ⅝". Make eight bundles and start gluing them around pistil.

3 Glue stamen pieces so they extend 5 mm / ¼" outside pistil. After gluing first stamen pieces, add second pieces across from first. Then, glue one stamen piece on either side. Add remaining pieces so they fill gaps. Make stamens circular in shape. Tie ⅓ length #26 wire around base once to bind.

4 Make leaves. Glue two leaf cloths together with soft-type glue. Sandwich the #28 wire between a pair of Leaf-A pieces, and also -C pieces. Sandwich #30 wire between a pair made up of Leaf-B pieces. Be careful not to stretch as you glue. Trim about 1 mm / 1/16" in from the edge.

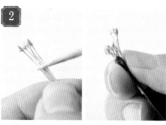

5 From base to tip, press Ultra-thin Single Groove brass tip. Match brass tip groove with wire and then move brass tip lengthwise over wire. Next, create five to six veins on each side.

6 Shape calyx cloth. Hot-press each segment up to notches, moving from edge inward.

7 Make petals. Glue two petal cloths together, *without* inserting wire. Trim off about 1–2 mm / 1/16" of the edge, regardless of misalignment. Fold in half lengthwise.

8 Unfold and stretch edge on both sides separately. At this point, the petal should curve a little.

9 Crumple up cloth, moving inward from tip.

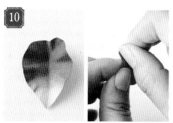

Stretch cloth to make frills.

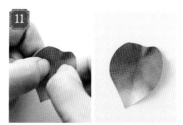

Next, pull cloth from center outward toward both sides to stretch.

Fold edge of petal inward. This completes the petal shaping. Instead of using a soldering iron, just use your fingers to shape.

Apply glue on base of Petal-a and attach to flower center from step **3**. Press cloth with fingers to attach securely.

Attach second Petal-a. Slightly overlap with first petal.

Place third Petal-a opposite from first and second petals.

Next, glue Petal-b pieces on while filling gaps between petals and flower stem. Glue as you gauge overall balance from the front.

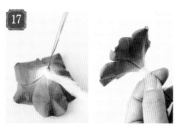

Tear cotton lengthwise into a thin strip. Apply small amount of glue to base of flower and wrap cotton around flower base. This makes a rosehip.

Adjust calyx cloth over cotton to make sure cotton fits snugly inside. If fit is okay, apply glue to calyx cloth and glue on base of flower, over cotton.

If calyx notch is shallow, make it deeper with scissors to prevent cotton fibers from protruding.

Tie a leftover wire (preferably #28 or #30) around the calyx and leave until it takes shape.

Layer two Leaf-B pieces on one Leaf-A piece and apply a small amount of glue at the base of these leaves.

Wrap with stem cloth. Apply glue slightly above bundle base and start binding wires with stem cloth.

After binding 15 mm / ⅝", bend one Leaf-B piece to the left and the other to the right.

Combine remaining two Leaf-B pieces below those from step 23. Bind with stem cloth for another 30 mm / 1⅛", then cut. Bend one Leaf-B piece left and the other right. This completes a five leaf branch.

Attach stipule cloth to branch from step 24. Apply glue to back side of branch and attach stipule cloth. Assemble Leaf-C pieces in a similar manner.

Undo wire at base of flower (step 20). Wrap stem cloth around flower stem from about 15 mm / ⅝" above the base. Bend flower stem so it is slightly tilted.

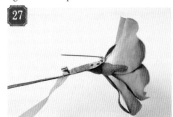

Leave stem cloth as is. Prepare a separate piece of stem cloth and attach a brooch pin (see p. 14). Do not bind brooch pin where it sits on rosehip.

After glue on brooch pin has completely dried, bend flower stem and resume binding with stem cloth. As you apply glue to stem cloth, bind twice. Bend flower stem to tilt flower downward.

Combine with Leaf-C branch and bind with stem cloth a few times.

Combine five leaf branch with stipule. Cut wire at 40 mm / 1½" from flower stem that was bent in step 28. Bind with stem cloth to complete.

Cut stem cloth 35 mm / 1⅜" down from end of brooch pin. Dispose of stem cloth end (see p. 14) to finish your Ramanas Rose brooch.

Lady Rose

Variety	Shrub Rose
Scientific Classification	*Roseae Rosa*
Blooming Period	Perpetual flowering

Instructions on p. 92

This fabric flower, Lady Rose, was made from a pattern cut from a real 'Lady Heirloom' rose with layered petals. 'Lady Heirloom' has a long, thin stem, but its blooms are packed with over a hundred petals. So, as the flowers bloom, the plant appears to be plunging toward the ground. The blooms maintain a cup shape and have a vanilla-like scent until they die.

About Pattern Making

Examining actual plants: touching, smelling, and even dissecting them to observe their structure. These are the steps I follow to make my fabric flower patterns.
When cut flowers aren't available, it's very rare but I might use dried or pressed flowers to make patterns. However, the end result always has a somewhat withered look. There is a subtle fineness in the withered look, but I personally prefer to make patterns from fresh, living plants whenever possible.

"Fabric flower botanical specimens" is what I call the items I make when applying my own procedure steps, meaning when I "observe the target plant." But that doesn't mean that the goal is always to "make it look like the real thing."

I believe that even if we are looking at the same thing, what we see is different for each individual. My desire is to replicate the beauty, loveliness, and delicateness of the plants I see. And also, to give form to things that are perhaps invisible to the average eye.

In the past, at a class I took to learn fabric flower making, four sepals were prepared to make a rose brooch. Even though I understood that it was designed to make wearing it as a brooch easy, I couldn't help but think, "the rose has five sepals . . ." I could never make fabric flowers as demonstrated by my teacher, so no matter what classes I took, I never did as well as the other students.

I do pattern making from scratch as much as possible every year. The reason is that I want to make fabric flowers as if encountering them for the first time each year. This makes me love my subjects more and more.

The "Lady Rose" is a "fabric flower botanical specimen" made from the 'Lady Heirloom' rose, which has the most densely layered petals of all the roses I grow. I will explain how to make a fabric flower pattern using this rose as an example.

When a flower has many petals, as with roses, arrange them in order of size. Start with the outer petals and just group them together if the petals are similar in size. These Lady Roses were grouped into five different sizes.

Among the various blooms on the plant, select the one whose overall form you want to capture and another one that has a similar blooming style. Carefully disassemble the secondary bloom and observe it while sketching and taking photographs. If a secondary bloom isn't available, disassemble only half of the primary bloom.

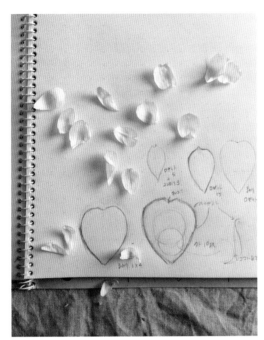

Sketch the target at actual size, in order to be able to reference the overall shape and appearance.

Select one petal of each size that has a nice shape and copy them. This makes for an original pattern. The original pattern for five different petals is shown in this photo. Note the characteristics of each petal group, like the number of petals and their shape. In a similar manner to the petals, copy the leaves and calyx.

The next step is to make a prototype. Carry out your work while the target is still alive if possible. If you can't make it right away, you can preserve your target flower through pressing and save it for later.

Making a prototype begins with the original pattern. Cut a piece of white cloth following your pattern. Shape the components using a soldering iron and assemble them as if you were making a test garment. Don't start prototyping with pure silk; instead use cotton or synthetic cloth that has a similar thickness. In most cases, the first prototype made directly from an actual flower doesn't work well.

If it is too thick when assembled, connect the petals in a circle or adjust the number of petals while considering the thickness of the fabric. If the plant is larger than the pattern when assembled, trim it down to 80% or 90% and try again. If you use fabric flower glue, the glue will peel off as soon as it is moistened with water. In addition, the parts that were ironed will flatten back out when moistened.

Once your prototype has reached the shape and size you envisioned you can apply water to separate each component and make them flat again. Then, transfer their shapes onto a piece of cardboard.

If you want to make a brooch, corsage, or other wearable item, you can go one step further and add a design. Use thicker fabric that is less likely to lose the shape of the flower. Reduce the number of petals while taking the fabric thickness into account, and consider what to omit and where to put the pin in your design.

Bourbon Rose

Variety	Bourbon Rose
Scientific Classification	*Roseae Rosa*
Blooming Period	Varies by cultivar

Instructions on p. 58

This spectacular rose, a descendant of an early Old Garden rose variety created by crossbreeding Eastern and Western roses, has sweetly scented blooms. The pattern for this silk flower is made from 'La Reine Victoria' and 'Madame Pierre Oger', which are Bourbon Rose varieties. They are climbing roses whose young blooms have a lovely round shape. 'La Reine Victoria' has bluish pink blooms and 'Madame Pierre Oger' has opal pink blooms. However, I decided to dye the petals apricot.

57

Materials

Stiffened cloth

Cotton lawn: Petal-a 10 pcs., Petal-b 15 pcs., Leaf-A 2 pcs., Leaf-B 4 pcs., Calyx 1 pc.
Extra-fine cotton: Petal-c 10 pcs., Petal-d 5 pcs.
Thin silk (*Usukinu*): Stem cloth

Styrene ball 15 mm / ⅝" diameter 1 pc.
Pips Small rose pip 30 pc., French pip 4 pc.
Jimaki wires
½ length green #26 1 pc., #28 1 pc., ½ length #28 1 pc., ½ length #30 2 pcs.
Brooch pin 30 cm / 11¾" wide 1 pc.
Cotton
Brass soldering tip types
9 mm / ⅜" Hemisphere, 15 mm / ⅝" Hemisphere, 21 mm / ¾" Hemisphere, Ultra-thin Single Groove

Dyeing

Beige (Brown + Sepia)
Apricot (Scarlet + Red + Brown + Sepia)
Leaf Green (Olive Green + Green + Brown)

Petals: Dye cotton lawn petal cloths in pairs. Dye extra-fine cotton petal cloth pieces separately. Dye pale Beige. Gradate Apricot from petal tip while cloth is damp. Add pale Leaf Green to petal base, drop in Beige to blend.
Leaf, Calyx: Dye uniformly Leaf Green. Add Beige to leaf base while still damp.
Stem cloth: Uniformly dye a piece of thin silk Leaf Green. Cut thin silk into 5 mm / ¼" wide strips (see p. 80).

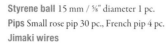

1 Shape petals on a soft sponge. Shape cotton lawn Petal-a pieces in pairs and -b in pairs. Use 9 mm / ⅜" Hemisphere brass tip to shape Petal-a. Forcefully press down on brass tip to round out. It's okay if cloth tucks under.

2 Use 15 mm / ⅝" Hemisphere brass tip to shape Petal-b, and -c. Use a 21 mm / ¾" Hemisphere brass tip to shape Petal-d. Shape same as Petal-a. Shape each Petal-c and -d cloth separately.

3 The petals should all be round now.

4 Apply glue to base of Petal-a and put the other Petal-a on while slightly shifting to right. Make five sets.

5 Thread #28 wire through styrene ball to make flower core (see p. 22). Put #26 wire through ball then around lower half of ball. Then, bind wire at bottom of ball. Just below ball, bind stem cloth around wire a few times.

6 Cover ball with glue and put one set of petals from step **4** on the ball.

7 Apply glue to base of second set of petals and attach while overlapping with first set of petals. Repeat in a counterclockwise direction.

8 After gluing on third set of petals, the ball should be completely covered. Apply glue to base of petals and attach fourth and fifth sets. Attach fifth set of petals by inserting edge under overlapping petals.

9 The petals overlap and layer around styrene ball.

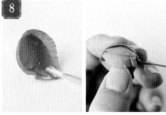

10

Make a layer of three Petal-b cloths. Apply glue to base of first Petal-b cloth. Put second Petal-b cloth on while shifting slightly to right. Next, attach third Petal-b cloth while shifting slightly to the left. Make five sets.

11

Continue to glue petals on ball where you left off. Apply glue to base of each Petal-b set and attach while shifting their position so that the five sets of Petal-b encase the flower.

12

Make a pair of Petal-c. Similar to Petal-a, lay a pair of Petal-c cloth pieces on top of each other. Shift top cloth slightly to the right and glue together. Make five sets.

13

Continue to glue petals on stem where you left off. Overlap petals in order to encase the flower with all five sets of Petal-c.

14

Apply glue to base of first Petal-d and attach from where you left off. Attach the second Petal-d while slightly overlapping the first Petal-d. Attach third Petal-d across from first and second.

15

Attach fourth and fifth Petal-d while filling gaps between first/third Petal-d and second/third Petal-d. The petal pieces are all on now.

16

Make the rosehip (see p. 51).

17

Insert #28 wire lengthwise inside a pair of Leaf-A pieces. Similarly, place #30 wire inside a pair of Leaf-B pieces and glue. Shape veins from front side (see p. 50), and then hot-press back side of leaf pieces between the veins, about 10 mm / ⅜" from the edge.

18

Combine one Leaf-A piece and two Leaf-B pieces to make a branch with three leaves (see pgs. 51–52). Bind wire with stem cloth for about 45 mm / 1¾".

19

Tilt flower slightly downward, then wrap stem cloth around wire for about 30 mm / 1¼" and stop. Attach brooch pin to stem using more stem cloth (see p. 52).

20

Resume wrapping stem cloth from step **19**. Combine branch with three leaves from step **18** at 45 mm / 1¾" below rosehip.

21

Wrap stem cloth farther, about 35 mm / 1⅜" down the stem. Then, trim off excess wire. Dispose of stem cloth end (see p. 14). Enjoy your completed Bourbon Rose brooch.

French Rose

Variety	*Rosa gallica*
Scientific Classification	*Roseae Rosa*
Blooming Period	Once-flowering

Instructions on p. 96

This is the oldest variety of Old Garden rose. The lobed sepals, and the way the petals gradually open from the rosette, along with their fading color as the bloom matures—every moment is beautiful. I grow 'Duchesse de Montebello' and 'Belle Isis', both French roses. Some people say that they have a similar look, but I find that they each have their own individual allure. The pattern for this project is created from these two separate roses and made into a brooch.

Rose

Roses aren't just pretty flowers.

My love of roses probably came about because of the influence of my favorite childhood book. How much I longed for the rose potpourri, inks, and handmade cologne introduced in that book!

The first rose I ever bought, when I was in high school, was a 'Blue Moon'. It grew well and produced many light purple flowers with a wonderful scent. I used the petals to make various things. However, due to a sudden move, I was not able to take the 'Blue Moon' with me. Unfortunately, my mother passed away a few years later as well. So, I was away from growing plants for a very long time.

In my late thirties, I left a career over a decade long in the arts and crafts field. At that time, when I had lost the desire to create anything, I suddenly wanted to visit my hometown. The house was still there, but there were no 'Blue Moon' in the flowerbed. Instead, there was just a hedge. As I headed home, I started to think to myself, "I would love to try growing roses again . . ."

And now I make fabric flowers *and* grow plants. Originally, I read books on how to grow roses and started with English roses, which seemed easy to grow. Now, I have about twenty pots of Old Garden roses and climbing roses. I grow them in pots and without using chemicals to the greatest extent possible. I make syrup and bath salts out of rose petals. And making new patterns every year is one of my greatest pleasures. I started Instagram just to show people pictures of the beautiful roses I grew.

When the rose buds start coming in, I become really impatient. I get up at sunrise and wait for the buds to unravel and the roses to bloom. Roses are beautiful at any time, but I think they are exceptionally beautiful when they are about to bloom or, strangely enough, when they are falling apart.

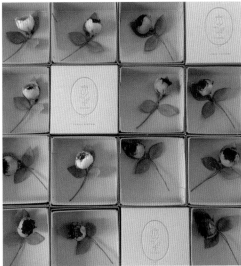

Rose Scents

Roses have an amazing variety of scents. The sweet, sweet Old Garden rose scent, a tea-like scent (sort of like opening a bag of loose-leaf tea), the fruity scent of apples or lemons, or the aroma of herbs and myrrh. At "rose" themed exhibitions I held, I always prepared salt infused with the scent of each variety of fabric rose I made, just so that people could enjoy their wonderful scent. The roses, reproduced in fabric, had the scent of their representative rose infused into them and it was wonderful.

It was a great pleasure to see that some people became interested in growing roses as a result of coming to these exhibitions. I really hope to do more exhibitions like that.

Rose Scent Infused Bath Salt
• Sea salt
• Rose petals from a freshly picked, recently bloomed rose (do not use the five outermost petals)

Boil a glass jar to sanitize it and then let it dry. Layer salt and rose petals in the jar. Place the glass jar in a cool and dark place to allow the scent to mature and infuse the salt.

Rose Shape

What I found interesting when I held my workshops was that the shape of the finished rose looked different for each participant, even if they used the same kit. The end result is truly a reflection of what each participant envisioned while they were making their own personal rose. It's so fascinating: those who love roses and grow and observe roses, tend to mimic the bloom types that they love. Personally, I believe that imaginative people create far more beautiful roses than people who rigidly follow instructions.

A few years ago, I held an exhibition on the theme "If I were a rose cultivator." It was fun just thinking of which flower shape goes well with which color, like green-eyed blooms. If I made a blue rose, what shape would the bloom be? The *shapes* came from actual roses, but figuring out what colors to use and how to assemble them was like an experiment that I wrapped into the actual creation. That being said, I always want my creations to obey the "laws of nature" as much as possible.

Wild Tulip

Scientific Name	*Tulipa*
Scientific Classification	*Liliaceae Tulipa*
Blooming Period	March through June

Instructions on p. 67

The tulip is a monocotyledonous plant, and its flowers basically come in multiples of three. The inside three pieces are the petals and the outside three pieces are the sepals. The petals of the double-flowered tulips are mutated stamens. A huge craze called "Tulip Mania" arose in the Netherlands in the 17th century. Wild tulips are small and possess a simple and delicate charm, different from the gorgeous large flowers produced by breeding like those in the Netherlands. How lovely to see an array of tulips that have their bulbs and roots still attached.

Materials

Stiffened cloth

Pure silk crepe de Chine #16: Petal-a 9 pcs., Petal-b 9 pcs.

Pure silk satin crepe #14: Sepal 3 pcs.

Cotton satin: Leaf-A 1 pc., Leaf-B 2 pcs., Leaf-C 1 pc.

Stem cloth 10 x 40 mm / ⅜" x 1⅝"

Thin silk (*Usukinu*): Bulb 14 to 16 pcs., Roots as necessary

Leaf backing 70 x 90 mm / 2¾" x 3½", Wire cloth

Styrene ball Styrene Ball 13 mm / ½" diameter 1pc., 20 mm / ¾" diameter 1 pc.

Jimaki wires

⅓ length green #26 1 pc., #28 1 pc., ⅓ length #30 4 pcs.

⅓ length white #30 4 pcs.

Brass soldering tip types

Medium Petal, Ultra-thin Single Groove, Single Groove Chrysanthemum, Triple Groove Chrysanthemum

Dyeing

Red (Red + Brown + Green)

Leaf Green (Olive Green + Green + Sepia)

Beige (Brown + Sepia)

Dark Brown (Brown + Sepia + Green)

Petals: After uniformly dying with Red, add Leaf Green at the base of the petal while the cloth is still damp.

Sepals: After uniformly dying Leaf Green, add pale Red to the tip and base.

Leaves: After uniformly dying Leaf Green, add Beige from the base of the leaf.

Leaf backing, Stem cloth: Uniformly dye a piece of thin silk with Leaf Green. Cut the silk into 5 mm / ¼" wide strips (see p. 80).

Bulb, Roots: Prepare cloth dyed Beige and Dark Brown. After they have dried, fold into four layers. Overlay the bulb pattern and cut out. For the roots, cut Beige dyed cloth into 6 mm / ¼" strips.

Shape the petals and sepals. Use a hard sponge and Medium Petal brass tip. Press the brass tip along the contours on the back.

Press Ultra-thin Single Groove brass tip, from base to tip, along the centerline.

Make flower core from 13mm / ½" diameter styrene ball with #28 wire (see p. 22). Apply glue to ball and attach three Petal-b pieces around the ball. The ball must not be visible from the top.

Apply glue to base of Petal-b cloth and glue on where the petals overlap. Glue three Petal-b pieces. Also, add remaining three Petal-b pieces in a similar manner.

Similar to Petal-b, glue on Petal-a so it looks like the petals are gradually opening.

Add sepals in a similar manner. Apply glue just on sepal base. Gauge overall balance as you go.

From the flower base, bind wire cloth downward for about 40 mm / 1⅝". Then, cover the wire cloth with stem cloth (see p. 8).

Line leaves with backing pieces. Glue the leaves on a piece of thin silk at an angle. Place the leaves at an angle. Once the glue has dried, cut out each leaf piece by cutting inside the outline.

Shape the leaves. Trace wire with brass tip on the back side.

Assemble flower and leaves. Apply about 10mm / ⅜" of glue to base of Leaf-B and attach to stem. Tilt flower a little.

Next, glue other Petal-B on opposite side. Glue Leaf-A on stem, slightly shifted away from Petal-B. Last, glue the Petal-C at back. As you glue the leaves on, add impressions to each leaf.

Prepare four strips of thin silk to make roots. On #30 white wire, start wrapping the thin silk strip 5 mm / ¼" down from wire tip. Wrap strip longer than wire and treat trailing strip as in the above photo.

Insert an awl deeply into 20 mm / ¾" diameter styrene ball. Apply glue to stem that will be hidden inside the ball. Then, insert stem into hole in ball. Trim off excess wire leaving about 10 mm / ⅜" from the ball.

Use pliers to bend wire ends into a U-shape. Push them into the ball.

Press ball down on a flat surface to make bottom flat.

Place bulb pattern on cloth and cut out. The cloth should be four layers. Cut out both light and dark colored bulb cloth.

Use Triple Groove Chrysanthemum brass tip to shape thin silk bulb cloth. On a hard sponge, hot-press a set of two bulb cloths, from edge to edge, to create a crease.

Apply glue on ball and begin attaching bulb cloths from the side.

Attach second cloth by overlapping half of the first cloth. Apply glue where cloth overlaps the ball.

Proceed to glue third and fourth pieces the same as the first and second. Continue until the ball is covered. It takes approximately seven to eight cloth pieces. Pinch bottom part to crumple a bit.

Glue on dark colored thin silk pieces, similar to the light colored ones.

Push cloths outward at the bottom of the bulb, and perforate four holes for inserting the roots with an awl.

Apply glue where wire isn't bound with root cloth and plug hole. Apply glue to ball and cover from bottom up as you put the bulb cloth between roots.

Wrap root piece around the awl to curl it.

Lightly pull curled roots and put them together.

Your Wild Tulip is complete.

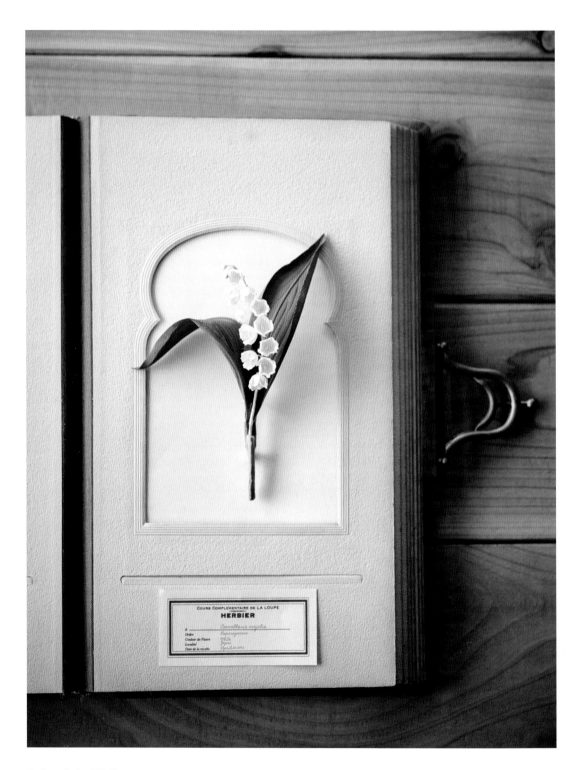

Lily of the Valley

Scientific Name	*Convallaria majalis*
Scientific Classification	*Asparagaceae Convallaria*
Blooming Period	April through May

Instructions on p. 98

The Lily of the Valley has small bell-like flowers. It usually has twelve to fourteen, but if you find one that has thirteen flowers, keep it! It is very rare and considered a good omen. Even since I heard that story from a florist in Hokkaido, I just can't help but count the number of flowers every time I see the wonderful lily of the valley. In France, the first of May is Le Jour du Muguet. It is customary to give lily of the valley, but it is also wonderful to give a fabric Lily of the Valley brooch along with your bouquet of real ones.

Snowdrop

Scientific Name	*Galanthus nivalis*
Scientific Classification	*Amaryllidaceae Galanthus*
Blooming Period	February through March

Instructions on p. 100

Awakening from beneath the snow the little Snowdrop heralds the arrival of spring. Snowdrops are plants that appear in the Russian fairy tale *The Twelve Months*. It is also known as the Candlemass Day (February 2) flower, or the Feast of Mary's Purification flower. The way they bloom in clusters in the forest makes it look like there is still a little snow on the ground. Let's create these tear-drop shaped, lustrous flowers using milky white, delicate silk.

Muscari

Scientific Name	*Muscari neglectum*
Scientific Classification	*Asparagaceae Muscari*
Blooming Period	March through May

Instructions on p. 102

Muscari blooms like a small bunch of grapes. There is also a cute variety that looks like it's wearing a pale light blue or white hat on its head. If the plant isn't properly cared for, its leaves will grow long and spindly. It should probably be dug up if it is in that shape, but honestly spindly leaves and smaller flowers are cute in their special way.

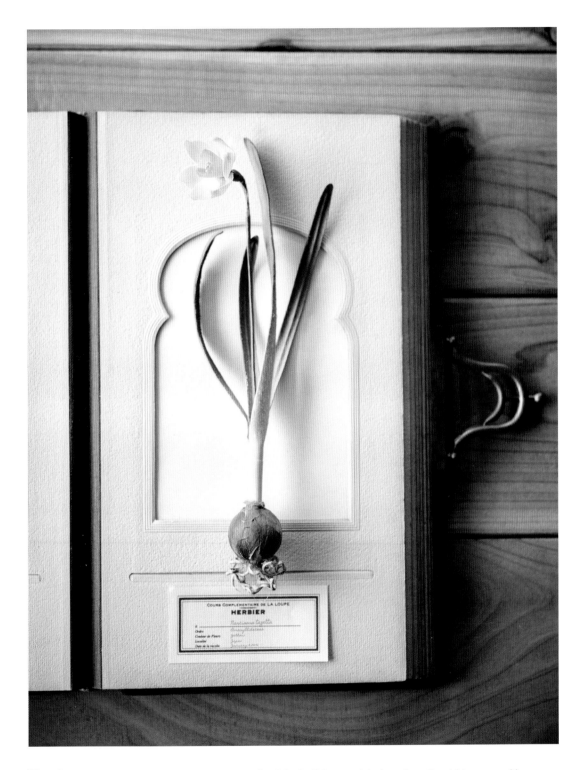

Narcissus

Scientific Name	*Cyclawineus*
Scientific Classification	*Amaryllidaceae Narcissus*
Blooming Period	November through April

Instructions on p. 104

When I think of Narcissus, it is always Jonquil—with its trumpet-like secondary corolla—that comes to my mind first. For this piece, however, I used a pattern that I had created using the small-flowered garden type 'Tête-à-tête.' The trumpet emerges from inside a bud wrapped carefully inside of the thin paper bag-like tepals. I carefully replicated the details of the flat stem and the remnants of the pouch-like tepals.

Tools

These are the tools that I regularly use. Everyone has their own preference, of course, so just use this section as a reference.

1. Ruler (a metal ruler that can be used with a rotary cutter)

2. Round nose pliers (flat nose pliers also come in handy)

3. Bamboo skewers   4. Awls (both regular and small blade width awls)

5. Tweezers   6. Eraser pencil

7. Mechanical pencil (both drafting and arts-and-crafts style)

8. Scissors (Separate pairs for cutting wires, for cutting thread and pips, and for cutting fabric)

9. Rotary cutter   10. Cutting mat   11. Hard sponge (a small sponge for punching holes)

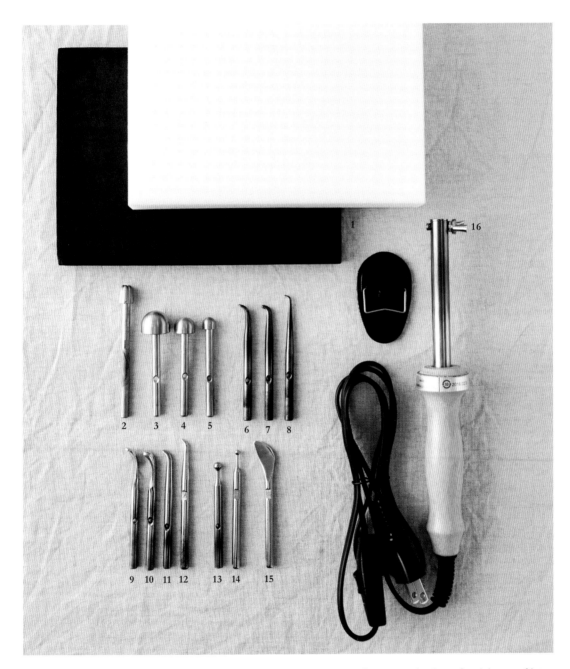

1. Ironing sponge: soft (white) and hard (black). (Used with the soldering iron. Cover the sponge with a thin, soft, tightly woven fabric to prevent burning. Choose soft or hard based on the brass tip you need. The instructions provided use a hard sponge unless otherwise noted.) Brass soldering tips: 2. Forget-me-not 3. 21 mm / ¾" Hemisphere 4. 15 mm / ⅝" Hemisphere 5. 9 mm / ⅜" Hemisphere 6. Triple Groove Chrysanthemum 7. Single Groove Chrysanthemum 8. Ultra-thin Single Groove Chrysanthemum 9. Large Petal 10. Medium Petal 11. Small Petal 12. Ultra-thin Petal 13. Large Lily of the Valley 14. Small Lily of the Valley 15. Line 16. Soldering iron and holder

CAUTION! The shaft at the end of the soldering iron is hot. If you touch it accidentally, you will get burned! Once the soldering iron is heated, it will remain hot for a while even after it is turned off. Frequently turn off the soldering iron during your work. Check its temperature by keeping a wet towel nearby and performing a dab test. The temperature is too low if you notice that the iron isn't producing enough effect. Adjust the temperature as you work on your project. Also, be sure to unplug the power supply, in addition to turning off the switch, if you ever leave the soldering iron unattended.

Materials

These materials can be purchased at fabric flower specialty stores, arts and crafts supply stores, or online.

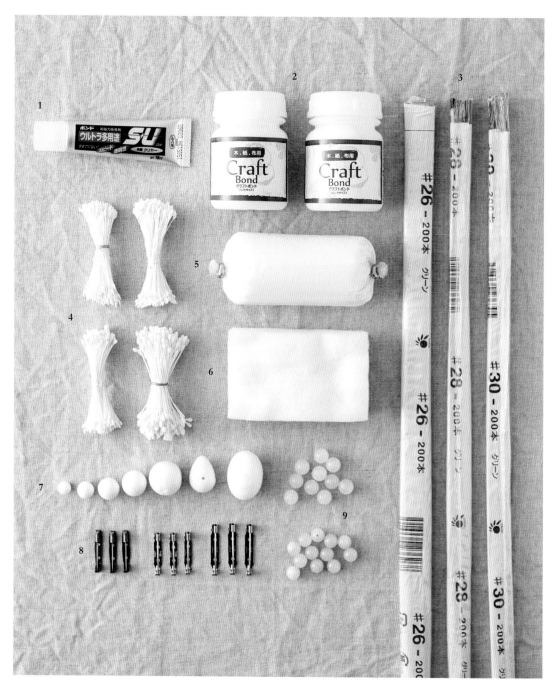

1. Multi-purpose glue   2. Floral PVA glue (soft-type and hard-type. Unless otherwise noted, use hard-type. Adjust both types to desired consistency.)   3. Jimaki wire (Japanese floral wire) (commonly used gauges: #26, #28, #30, and also #22, #24, #33. Use green colored wires unless otherwise noted.)   4. Stamens of various sizes and with a variety of pips.   5. Polymer clay (for making bulbs and flower centers)   6. Cotton   7. Styrene balls (various sizes and shapes)   8. Brooch pin (use your preferred color)   9. Gemstone beads (For berries found on Mistletoe; glass beads can also be used)

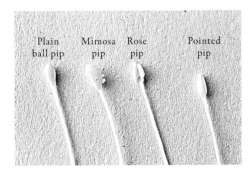

Plain ball pip | Mimosa pip | Rose pip | Pointed pip

These are the stamens used to make the center of a flower.
There are several different types of stamen ends, or pips, available. Choose based on your flower's needs.

*The projects here use starched fabrics. Prepare your cotton and silk by starching them very heavily to make them stiff. If you use synthetic fabrics, they'll require less starch to create the same degree of stiffness. Choose thin silk (*usukinu*), which is easier to wrap around wire, for strips of stem cloth.

Stiffened cloth
Synthetic
1. Thin silk (*Usukinu*) 2. Poplin 3. Crepe de Chine
4. Thin crepe rayon

Cotton
5. Cotton lawn 6. 15000 cotton (hard starched, Can be substituted by Cotton lawn) 7. Extra-fine cotton 8. Cotton satin
9. Super-fine velvet

Pure Silk
10. Pure silk georgette #6   11. Pure silk satin crepe #10
12. Pure silk satin crepe #14   13. Pure silk habutai #8
14. Pure silk habutai #10   15. Pure silk crepe de Chine #10
16. Pure silk crepe de Chine #14   17. Pure silk crepe de Chine #16

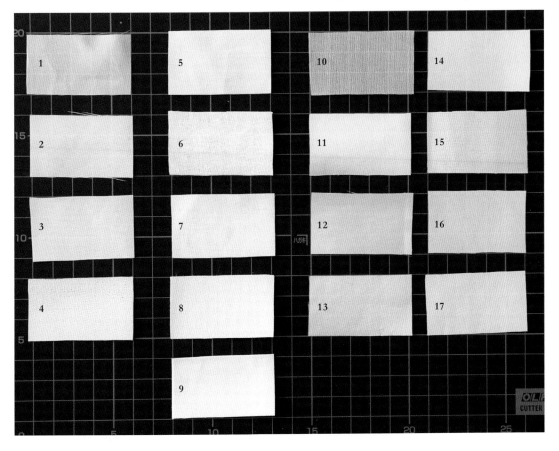

Dyeing

Use a dye that is closest to your intended color as the base. Mix other dyes in little by little. Be careful not to mix too many dyes, as this will reduce saturation and produce a muddy look.

1. Brush and hake brush (Use a different brush for dark colors and light colors.) 2. Enamel cup, enamel container, glass jar (Use white containers that show colors clearly. Choose transparent containers for storing dye.) 3. Dye (Use direct dyes. One brand is iDye from Jacquard Products. Also, W. Cushing & Co. has a line of direct dyes called Perfection Direct Dyes.) 4. Poster color (or Liquitex) 5. Denatured alcohol (Used to dye pips. Highly flammable! Handle with care.) COPIC Markers (Alcohol-based ink markers. Convenient when dyeing small numbers of pips.) 7. Lab spoon 8. Flat nosed tweezers 9. Measuring spoons (Aside from a tablespoon and teaspoon, you need measuring spoons that can measure from 1cc to $\frac{1}{10}$ cc.)

Dyeing: French Hydrangea

Cutting the Cloth

Prepare stiffened cloth, mechanical pencil, stapler, small-sized quilting pins, scissors, etc. Cut the cloth in two layers (cut thin cloth in four layers and cut heavy nap cloth in one layer).

Place pattern on cloth and trace. For complex patterns or patterns that are cut radially, you can place the pattern under the cloth and just trace over it.

Staple around cloth to prevent shifting when cutting. When cutting intricate patterns, use quilting pins to hold the cloth in several places. Staple center of pattern when pattern has radial cuts, as with white clover.

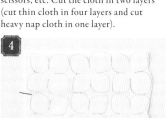

Trace pattern. Keep spacing tight so you don't waste cloth. Keep remnants and store them according to cloth type, as scraps can be used later to test dye colors.

Cut inside traced line with scissors. Keep cut pieces together if they need to be dyed in pairs.

Mixing Dyes

Important:
Prepare dye solution according to instructions provided with the chosen dye.

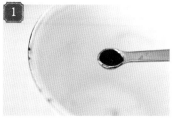

Put dye in cup.

Add hot water to dissolve dye.

Turquoise Blue, Blue, Green, Sepia, and (not shown) Brown dyes are ready. Dye a piece of remnant cloth to confirm color.

Create main French Hydrangea color by adding other colors to Turquoise Blue (base color).

Each time you add a color, dye a piece of remnant cloth to check newly created color. Sort remnants according to cloth type. Be sure to use the same type of remnant cloth as the cloth used in your project to test dye color. Be sure to check color *after* the cloth has dried.

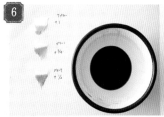

Add Green and Sepia. The key is to create a color that is more saturated than what you envision.

Create all the colors you need as shown here.

Dyeing: Gradation

Dye French Hydrangea florets. The leftmost is dyed in Gray Beige. Dye the florets by layering colors. The photo shows colors when cloth is still wet. Colors becomes lighter once the cloth has dried completely.

Add a small amount of Dark Brown and Brown in a bowl of hot water. Then, take some of your main dye color, by dipping a brush in it, and add it to the bowl to make Gray Beige. Pick up a pair of petal cloths with tweezers and submerge them in the bowl.

Place the floret cloths (from **2**) on a piece of paper that is sitting on some newspaper. After moisture has evaporated to a certain extent, dip a brush in the main color and dye floret cloths. Leave some edges untouched.

Take Dull Green (see p. 12) and brush over the untouched areas from **3**.

Add Grape dye to the floret cloths in the same manner as the previous step. Let dry, check color, and add or layer more color to achieve the exact color you envisioned. Confirm that the dye has penetrated to back side of cloth.

Dyeing: Submerging

Pick up cloth with tweezers and submerge in dye. Let the dye penetrate cloth.

Dyeing: Uniform Color

For this method you dye cloth without cutting. Prepare dye in a shallow container. Dip cloth in dye, beginning with edge, then pull edge forward so the rest of the cloth dips into the dye. Spread wet cloth on newspaper to remove excess dye. This will create a finish without unevenness.

To make stem cloth, after it's dried, fold it. Then, cut cloth in 5 mm / ¼" wide strips using a rotary cutter.

Dyeing Stamens/Pips

Dilute dye with a small amount of hot water. Add denatured alcohol (because too much water will dissolve the pip head). Soak pip head in dye to test color. Once dye has reached the intended color, bundle about ten stamens together and dip in dye.

Remove them quickly and dry off excess moisture on a piece of paper towel. If the color is lighter than you expected, let dry completely and then repeat dyeing process.

It is useful to make a color swatch with the color recipe you just used, along with a dyed sample cloth, to capture each of your colors for future reference. Put remaining dye in storage bottles, label, and store in a cool, dark place.

Instructions

* Refer to basic instructions on the earlier pages for each project.
* The unit of measurement is primarily mm. This book also provides measurements in inches; however, they are only approximate conversions.
* All cloth is dyed prior to assembling. Please use the provided dye combinations as a reference, but be sure to create your own desired colors.
* Pips are often made from materials like flour and cornstarch. They will easily melt in water, so remove them from any dye as quickly as possible. Use COPIC marker instead of dye when coloring fewer than ten.
* In most cases, cut each component on the fabric bias.
* When using a soldering iron, cover the sponge with fabric. See page 75.
* When gluing cloth together, be careful not to get any glue on the front side.
* As you assemble components, observe both front and back of the plant. Consider the overall balance.
* Brooch pins aren't attached to bulkier fabric flowers. Just enjoy them as ornamental pieces.

COURS COMPLÉMENTAIRE DE LA LOUPE
HERBIER

à
Ordre
Couleur de Fleurs
Localité
Date de la récolte

p. 16 Round Leaf Eucalyptus

Materials

Stiffened cloth

Extra-fine cotton: Leaf-A, -B, -C, and -D 4 pcs. each

Super-fine velvet: Leaf-D backing 1 pc., Brooch pin backing 1 pc.

Thin silk (*Usukinu*): Stem cloth

Pips

Small or ultra-small rose pip 1 pc. Cut in half after dyeing.

Jimaki wires

½ length green #26 1 pc., ⅓ length #28 2 pcs., ⅓ length #30 6 pcs.

Brooch pin

25 mm / 1" wide 1 pc.

Brass soldering tip type

Large Petal, Line

Dyeing

Leaf Green (Green + Brown + Sepia)

Beige (Brown + Sepia)

Leaf-A -B, -C -D: Dye in pairs. After uniformly dyeing Pale Beige, dye Leaf Green while still damp. Drop Beige at base and gradate.

Leaf-D backing, Brooch pin backing: Dye each cloth separately. Dye uniformly with Leaf Green.

Stem cloth: Uniformly dye a piece of thin silk with Leaf Green. Cut into 5 mm / ¼" wide strips (see p. 80).

Pip: Dye a green that is close to leaf color.

Brooch pin backing

Pip

Leaf-A

Leaf-B

Leaf-C

Brooch pin

Leaf-D backing

Leaf-D

Stem

Hot-press Diagram

Use Line brass tip on both sides.

Large Petal brass tip

Large Petal brass tip

Line brass tip

Leaf-A

Leaf-B, -C, -D

Full Size Pattern

Leaf-A: 4 pcs.

Leaf-B: 4 pcs.

Leaf-C: 4 pcs.

Leaf-D: 4 pcs.
Leaf-D backing: 1 pc.

Brooch pin backing: 1 pc.

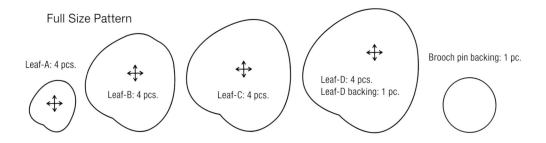

Steps

1. Sandwich a ⅓ length wire between pair of dyed leaf cloths and glue together. For Leaves-A, -B, and -C use #30 wire and Leaf-D uses #28 wire.
2. Glue backing cloth to back of one Leaf-D piece. Trim off misaligned edges.
3. Use Large Petal brass tip to produce a gentle curve (in reality Eucalyptus leaves aren't roundish, this is done to produce a nuanced look). Hot-press Line brass tip along both sides of wire on Leaf-A. Hot-press Leaf-B, -C, and -D in the same manner as Leaf-A, but add three to four veins.
4. Sandwich ½ length #26 wire between two pips that have been cut in half. Glue together. Then, bind with stem cloth once.
5. Combine two Leaf-A pieces, facing each other, on stem from step 4. Bind with stem cloth while carefully covering Leaf-A wires. After covering about halfway down the wires on Leaf-A, combine two Leaf-B pieces facing each other. Similarly, combine Leaf-C and -D pieces facing each other.
6. After combining all leaf pieces, make stem 30–40 mm / 1¼"–1½" long and trim off excess. Cover stem with stem cloth.
7. Apply glue evenly to back side of brooch pin backing cloth. Place on inside of pin. Then, attach to backing cloth of Leaf-D.
8. Curl leaves outward and add a gentle curve to the stem.

4, 5

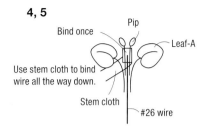

As you bind wires with stem cloth, combine leaves so they face each other on the stem.

7

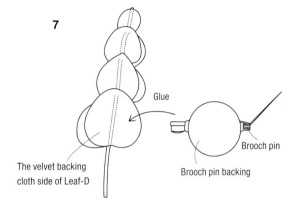

p. 17   Pattern: Eucalyptus with Buds

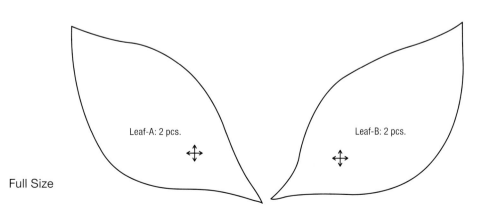

Leaf-A: 2 pcs.

Leaf-B: 2 pcs.

Full Size

p. 34 Edelweiss

Materials

Stiffened cloth
Super-fine velvet: Bract-A 3 pcs., Bract-B 2 pcs., Leaf-C 2 pcs., Leaf-D 1 pc., Stem cloth 12 x 78 mm / ½" x 3"

Brooch pin backing 10 x 30 mm / ⅜" x 1¼"

Thin silk (*Usukinu*): Wire wrap, Backing 40 x 150 mm / 1½" x 5⅞"

Jimaki wires
⅓ length white #26 1 pc., ¼ length #30 5 pcs., ½ length #35 6 pcs.

Brooch pin
25 mm / 1" wide 1 pc.

Sewing thread
Cotton
Brass soldering tip type
Ultra-thin Single Groove

Dyeing

Leaf Green (Green + Brown + Sepia)
Beige (Sepia + Brown)
Yellow (Yellow + Sepia)

Bract, Leaf: Dye each cloth separately. Uniformly dye a very pale Beige. Drop pale Leaf Green at base and gradate.

Stem cloth, Brooch pin backing: Dye pale Leaf Green (same color as thin silk backing).

Backing, Wire cloth: Use pale Leaf Green to uniformly dye a piece of thin silk in the same manner as the stem cloth. Cut into 5 mm / ¼" wide strips (see p. 80).

Sewing thread: Uniformly dye thread with Yellow and pale Beige (similar to the bract). Wring the thread lightly to remove excess moisture, then use paper towel to dry well.

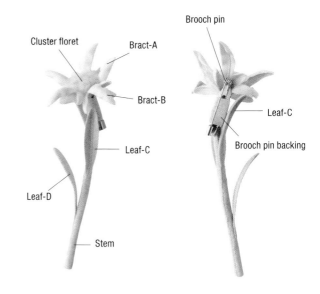

Brooch pin

Cluster floret

Bract-A

Bract-B

Leaf-C

Leaf-C

Brooch pin backing

Leaf-D

Stem

Hot-press Diagram

Leaf-C, -D

Bract-A, -B

Trace wire with Ultra-thin Single Groove brass tip on back side.

Ultra-thin Single Groove brass tip

Ultra-thin Single Groove brass tip

Full Size Pattern

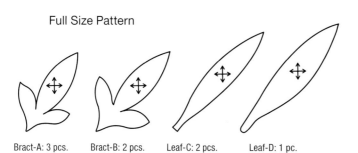

Bract-A: 3 pcs.   Bract-B: 2 pcs.   Leaf-C: 2 pcs.   Leaf-D: 1 pc.

Steps

1. Make the bracts and leaves. Spread a thin layer of glue on back side of bract and leaves. Glue them on a piece of thin silk. Insert ¼ length #30 wire between bract cloth and thin silk.

2. Shape veins on bract piece as shown in the diagram using Ultra-thin Single Groove brass tip. Trim off wire at 5 mm / ¼" from base of bract.

3. Make clustered florets using sewing thread. Cut beige and yellow thread 50 mm / 2" long. Cut several pieces. Layer yellow threads on beige. Bind at center with a ½ length #35 wire and fold bundle in half. Bind wire cloth at base of fold. Trim off thread bundle to a length of 3–4 mm / ⅛". You'll need one central clustered floret and five small clustered florets around it. Use twenty-four 50 mm / 2" long beige threads and twenty 50 mm / 2" long yellow threads to make a 5–6 mm / ¼" diameter central clustered floret. Use eighteen 50 mm / 2" long beige threads and ten 50 mm / 2" long yellow threads to make five sets of 3–4 mm / ⅛" diameter clustered florets.

4. Apply glue to tip of ⅓ length #26 wire and attach to central clustered floret. Add small clustered florets around the central one and bind together. Make wires 75 mm / 3" long and trim off excess. Bind wires with wire cloth. Apply glue at base of clustered florets and cover groups with a thin layer of cotton fibers.

5. Apply glue to base of bract pieces. Attach them around groups of clustered florets in the following order: Bract-A, -B, -A, -A, -B.

6. Wrap stem cloth lengthwise on stem.

7. Tilt base of flower slightly forward. Attach brooch pin to back side below flower base using wire cloth. Cover wire cloth with brooch pin backing cloth and trim off excess.

8. Apply glue at base of leaf cloth on back side and attach three leaves on stem.

1

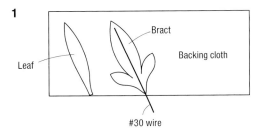

Leaf

Bract

Backing cloth

#30 wire

2

5mm / ¼"

3

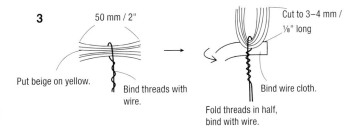

50 mm / 2"

Put beige on yellow.

Bind threads with wire.

Fold threads in half, bind with wire.

Cut to 3–4 mm / ⅛" long

Bind wire cloth.

4

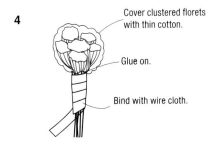

Cover clustered florets with thin cotton.

Glue on.

Bind with wire cloth.

Materials

Stiffened cloth

Cotton lawn: Corolla 7 pcs.

Extra-fine cotton: Leaf-A, -B, -C 2 pcs. each

Thin silk (*Usukinu*): Stem cloth

Jimaki wires

⅓ length green #26 1 pc., ⅓ length #28 5 pcs.

Brooch pin

25 mm / 1" wide 1 pc.

White acrylic paint

Brass soldering tip type

Ultra-thin Single Groove

Dyeing

Leaf Green (Olive Green + Brown + Sepia)

Beige (Brown + Sepia)

Corolla: Dye in pairs. Uniformly dye very pale Beige. For six out of seven corolla cloths, once excess moisture has evaporated, drop Leaf Green at center and gradate.

Uniformly dye remaining cloth pale Leaf Green.

Leaf: Dye in pairs. Uniformly dye Leaf Green. Once excess moisture has evaporated, add Beige to base.

Stem cloth: Uniformly dye a piece of thin silk with Leaf Green. Cut into 5 mm / ¼" wide strips (see p. 80).

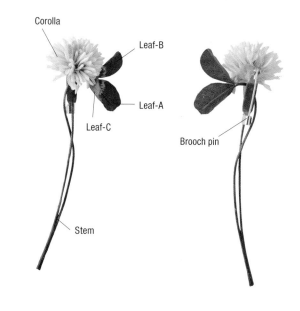

Corolla

Leaf-B

Leaf-A

Leaf-C

Brooch pin

Stem

Hot-press Diagram

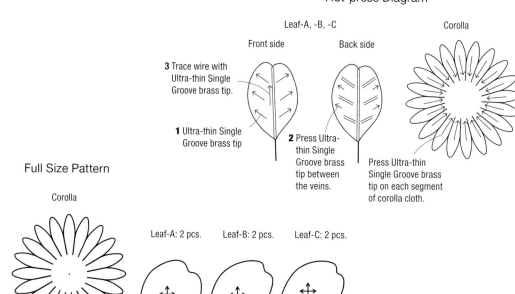

Leaf-A, -B, -C

Front side

Back side

Corolla

3 Trace wire with Ultra-thin Single Groove brass tip.

1 Ultra-thin Single Groove brass tip

2 Press Ultra-thin Single Groove brass tip between the veins.

Press Ultra-thin Single Groove brass tip on each segment of corolla cloth.

Full Size Pattern

Corolla

Leaf-A: 2 pcs.   Leaf-B: 2 pcs.   Leaf-C: 2 pcs.

Steps

1. Put ⅓ length #28 wire between a pair of leaf cloths that were dyed together. Glue them together.
2. Hot-press on front side to add veins. Then, from the back side, hot-press between the veins to add lines. With the front side facing up, hot-press over the wire from base to leaf tip.
3. Paint patterns on leaf pieces using white acrylic. After the paint has dried, combine three leaf pieces and bind wires with stem cloth.
4. Hot-press corolla cloth from center outward.
5. Drop a small amount of glue on base of each segment of corolla cloth and twist.
6. Bend tip of a ⅓ length #26 wire with pliers.
7. Perforate center corolla cloth piece that has been dyed Leaf Green. Thread wire from step 6 through cloth.
8. Do the same for remaining corolla cloths to attach to wire.
9. Add two ⅓ length #28 wires and bind with stem cloth. Add leaf component and bind stems together. Trim off excess wires and cover ends with stem cloth.
10. Tilt flower forward. Attach brooch pin at back.
11. Adjust position of leaves as desired.

3

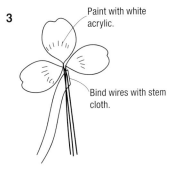

Paint with white acrylic.

Bind wires with stem cloth.

5

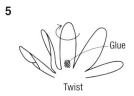

Glue

Twist

7

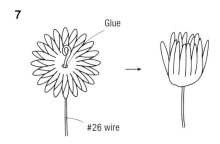

Glue

#26 wire

p. 40 Sweet Violet

Materials

Stiffened cloth

Pure silk crepe de Chine #16: Corolla 2 pcs., Bud 1 pc.

Cotton lawn: Leaf-A, -B, -C, 2 pcs. each, Calyx 3 pcs.

Thin silk (*Usukinu*): Stem cloth, Spur cloth 8 x 50 mm / ¼" x 2"

Pips

Pointed pips or ultra-small point ball pip 2 pcs.

Jimaki wires

⅓ length green #28 3 pcs., 140 mm / 5½" length green #28 3 pcs., #30 1 pc.

Brooch pin

25 mm / 1" wide 1 pc.

Black-purple acrylic paint

Cotton

Brass soldering tip type

Ultra-thin Petal, Forget-me-not

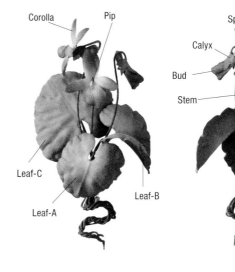

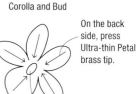

Dyeing

Violet (Violet + Red Violet + Blue + Brown)
Beige (Sepia + Brown)
Leaf Green (Olive Green + Green + Sepia)

Corolla, Bud: Dye each piece separately. After uniformly dyeing pale Beige, gradate Violet from the edges while still damp. Drop pale Leaf Green at center. After cloth has completely dried, paint lines of stria on lower corolla petals using acrylic paint.

Uniformly dye remaining cloth pale Leaf Green.

Leaf: Dye in pairs. After uniformly dyeing pale Beige, add Leaf Green—moving in from edges— while still damp. Gradate toward center. Also, gradate Beige from center outward.

Calyx: Uniformly dye each cloth, one at a time, Leaf Green.

Spur: Uniformly dye with Violet.

Pip: Dye orangish yellow.

Stem cloth: Uniformly dye a piece of thin silk with Leaf Green. Cut into 5 mm / ¼" wide strips (see p. 80).

Hot-press Diagram

Leaf

On the back side, press Forget-me-not brass tip.

Corolla and Bud

On the back side, press Ultra-thin Petal brass tip.

On the front side, press down Ultra-thin Petal brass tip, but just on the flower cloth.

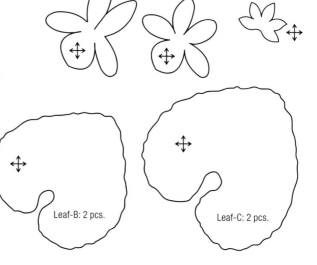

Corolla: 2 pcs.

Bud: 1 pc.

Calyx: 3 pcs.

Full Size Pattern

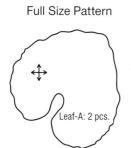

Leaf-A: 2 pcs.

Leaf-B: 2 pcs.

Leaf-C: 2 pcs.

Steps

1. Sandwich ⅓ length #28 wire between two dyed leaf cloths and glue together. Cut wire to 90 mm / 3½" long and wrap with stem cloth.
2. Firmly press Forget-me-not brass tip on back side of leaf, moving from outside to inside.
3. Press Ultra-thin Petal brass tip on back side of flower corolla, moving from tip of each segment towards the center. With the front side facing up, press the brass tip at the center. Do the same for the bud, except press from the front.
4. Cut a pip stem 10 mm / ⅜" long. Add 140 mm / 5½" long #28 wire to the pip and bind with stem cloth. Make three sets.
5. As shown in the figure at right, bend pip wire from step 4 to make a "spur" where nectar is collected. Stuff a piece of cotton inside to create volume.
6. Cover spur with a piece of thin, Violet dyed silk.
7. Combine flower corolla with pip set from step 5. Apply glue to base of pip head and wire. Insert pip head between two upper segments and pinch glued area with cloth. Adjust position of corolla using tweezers and attach calyx cloth to cover the flower stem and spur.
8. Combine bud with pip set from step 6. Same as step 7. Apply glue to pip set and insert pip head between two upper segments. Make sure bud covers pip head. Calyx should cover flower stem and spur.
9. Curve stems, as shown in figure at right. Combine two flower pieces with bud piece. Add Leaf-C at back, Leaf-B on side, and Leaf-A at front.
10. Bind with #30 wire and trim off excess wire. Bind stem cloth twice where stems are bound. Then attach brooch pin.
11. Twist stems under brooch pin to make them look like roots.

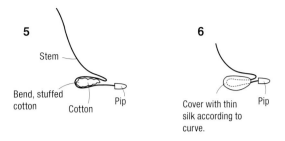

5

Stem

Bend, stuffed cotton

Cotton

Pip

6

Cover with thin silk according to curve.

Pip

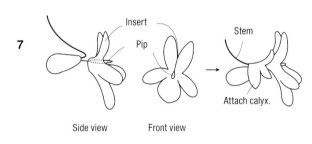

7

Insert

Pip

Stem

Attach calyx.

Side view

Front view

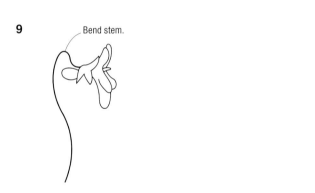

9

Bend stem.

Materials

Stiffened cloth
Cotton satin: Leaf 16 pcs.

Thin silk (*Usukinu*): Stem cloth

Round-shape bead
Diameter of 8 mm / ¼" 5 pcs. (Gemstones, glass beads, etc. Use desired color)

Pips
Medium to large rose pip 12 pcs. After dyeing, cut stem in half.

Jimaki wires
½ length green #26 4 pcs., ⅓ length #28 8 pcs., 40 mm / 1½" long #28 5 pcs., #30 3 pcs.

Brooch pin
25 mm / 1" wide 1 pc.

Clear multi-purpose adhesive

Brass soldering tip type
Triple Groove Chrysanthemum brass tip

Dyeing

Leaf Green (Olive Green + Green + Brown)
Accent Color (Brown + Sepia)

Leaf: Dye in pairs. Uniformly dye pale Accent Color. Then, dye Leaf Green while the cloth is still damp. Add Accent Color at base while cloth isn't completely dry.

Stem cloth: Uniformly dye a piece of thin silk Leaf Green. Cut into 5 mm / ¼" wide strips (see p. 80).

Pip: Dye Beige.

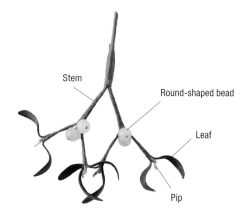

Stem

Round-shaped bead

Leaf

Pip

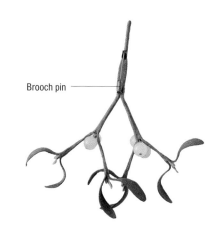

Brooch pin

Hot-press Diagram

Leaf

On the front side, trace wire with Triple Groove Chrysanthemum brass tip.

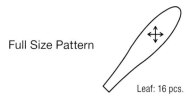

Full Size Pattern

Leaf: 16 pcs.

Steps

1. Sandwich ⅓ length #28 wire between a pair of leaf cloths that were dyed together. Glue together.
2. Hot-press Triple Groove Chrysanthemum brass tip upward from leaf tip.
3. Bend 6–7 mm / ¼" from tip of 40 mm / 1½" long #28 wire (see figure).
4. Apply multi-purpose adhesive where the wire is bent. Thread bead to make a berry on mistletoe. (If #28 wire is too tight for the bead, use #30 instead.) Thread all beads on wires.
5. Combine berries from step 4 with #30 wire. Make a bundle of two beads and a bundle of three beads. Bind wires on each bundle with stem cloth.
6. Glue three pips that have their stems cut in half around the #26 wire. Bind wire and pip stems with stem cloth for about 10 mm / ⅝".
7. Apply glue on base of leaf pieces and attach one leaf piece on each side of pip head from step 6. Wrap stem cloth downward for about 25 mm / 1".
8. Combine two leaf stems from step 7 with the berry stem from step 5 to make a Y-shape. Use berry stem as base. Bind with stem cloth for 25–30 mm / 1–1¼".
9. Put two branches from step 8 together, making a Y-shape. Bind the stems with #30 wire. Make the stem 40–45 mm / 1½"–1¾" long and trim off excess. Bind stems with stem cloth and cover ends with stem cloth.
10. Attach brooch pin to back side of stem from step 9 with another piece of stem cloth. Angle the leaves to produce "movement."

4

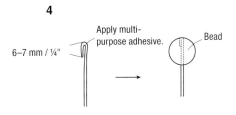

6–7 mm / ¼"

Apply multi-purpose adhesive.

Bead

5

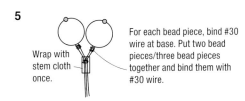

Wrap with stem cloth once.

For each bead piece, bind #30 wire at base. Put two bead pieces/three bead pieces together and bind them with #30 wire.

6

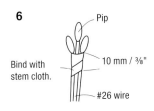

Bind with stem cloth.

Pip

10 mm / ⅜"

#26 wire

p. 53 Lady Rose

Materials

Stiffened cloth

Pure silk crepe de Chine #8: Petal-a 9 pcs., Petal-b
16 pcs., Petal-d 25 pcs.

Pure silk habutai #10: Peta-c 25 pcs., Petal-e 5 pcs.,
Petal-f 25 pcs.

Pure silk satin crepe #10: Petal-d 25 pcs.

Pure silk crepe de Chine #10: Petal-e 20 pcs.

B/B crepe de Chine: Leaf-A 4 pcs., Leaf-B 2 pcs.,
Leaf-C 2 pcs., Calyx 2 pcs.

Stipule-D 1 pc., Stipule-E 2 pcs.

Thin silk (*Usukinu*): Stem cloth

Pips

Small rose pip 13 pcs. After dyeing, cut stem in
half.

Ultra-small rose pip 15pcs. After dyeing, glue five
pips together and cut the stem to 15 mm / ⅝" long.
Make six sets.

Jimaki wires

½ length green #26 3 pcs., ½ length #28 11 pcs.,
#30 2 pcs.

Styrene ball

25 mm / 1" diameter 1 pc.

Cotton

Brass soldering tip types

Single Groove Chrysanthemum, Triple Groove
Chrysanthemum, Ultra-thin Single Groove, 9 mm
/ ⅜" Hemisphere, 15 mm / ⅝" Hemisphere, 21 mm
/ ¾" Hemisphere

Sponge

Hard sponge: Triple Groove Chrysanthemum brass
tip on petal cloths.

Soft sponge: Single Groove Chrysanthemum brass
tip and Hemisphere brass tips on petal cloths.

Dyeing

Rose (Pink + Brown + Green)

Beige (Sepia + Brown)

Yellow Brown (Yellow + Sepia)

Leaf Green (Olive Green + Green + Brown)

Petals: Uniformly dye very pale Beige. Then, while
still damp, uniformly dye Petal-a pieces Rose.
Then, gradate Rose on Petal-b, -c, -d and -f. Drop
Yellow Brown at base of petal cloths. Dye the outer
larger petal cloths pale Rose so that the outer petals
are paler.

Leaf, Calyx, Stipule: Uniformly dye Leaf Green
and drop Beige at base.

Stem cloth: Uniformly dye a piece of
thin silk Leaf Green. Cut into 5 mm /
¼" wide strips (see p. 80).

Pip: Dye yellow.

Petal-a, -b, -c, -d, -e, -f

Stipule-E

Leaf-A

Leaf-C

Stem

Leaf-B

Rosehip

Calyx

Stipule-D

Hot-press Diagram

Petal-a

Firmly, Ultra-thin Single Groove brass tip

Petal-b

Single Groove Chrysanthemum brass tip

Petal-d

1 On edge, Triple Groove Chrysanthemum brass tip

2 On back side, 21 mm / ¾" Hemisphere brass tip. Make round.

Pure silk habutai: Petal-f, -e

1 On edge, Triple Groove Chrysanthemum brass tip

2 On back side, 21 mm / ¾" Hemisphere brass tip. Make round.

Petal-c

1 On edge, Triple Groove Chrysanthemum brass tip

2 On back side, 21 mm / ¾" Hemisphere brass tip. Make round.

2 Triple Groove Chrysanthemum brass tip

Pure silk crepe de Chine: Petal-e

2 On back side, 9 mm / ⅜" Hemisphere brass tip

1 21 mm / ¾" Hemisphere brass tip

Leaf-C

2 Ultra-thin Single Groove brass tip

1 Ultra-thin Single Groove brass tip. Trace wire.

3 On back side, Ultra-thin Single Groove brass tip between veins.

Calyx

Leaf-A, -B

2 Ultra-thin Single Groove brass tip

2 Ultra-thin Single Groove brass tip

Ultra-thin Single Groove brass tip

Steps

1. Refer to diagram and shape petals accordingly. Shape Petals -a, -b, -c, -d, and -e in pairs. Shape pure silk crepe de Chine #10 Petal-e and Petal-f separately.

2. Make flower center (see p. 50, Instructions: Ramanas Rose). Add ½ length #26 wire and bind top once.

3. Glue five Petal-a pieces around flower center from step 2.

4. Layer three Petal-b pieces and one Petal-a piece while shifting lengthwise. Glue them together at base. Make four sets. Glue each set on stem around petals from step 3.

5. Layer four Petal-c cloths and one Petal-b cloth shifting widthwise (see p. 59 Bourbon Rose). Make four sets. Glue each set on the stem around the petals form step 4.

6. Layer five Petal-d pieces (mixing Pure silk habutai #8 and pure silk satin crepe #10) and one Petal-c cloth, shift widthwise, and glue together. Make four sets. Glue each set on stem around petals from step 5. Glue on ten Petal-d separately to fill gaps between petals.

7. Layer two Petal-f pure silk habutai #10 pieces, shift widthwise (see p. 58 Bourbon Rose), and glue together. Make eight sets. Glue each set on stem around petals from step 6. While checking overall balance, glue on remaining nine Petal-f pieces one at a time.

8. For the five Petal-e pure silk habutai #10 pieces, fold edge of petal over with your fingers. Then, glue one petal at a time around petals from step 7, while slightly lowering position each time.

9. While further lowering petal position, glue ten Petal-e pure silk crepe de Chine #10 pieces on one petal at a time. The bloomed rose is now complete.

10. Make a young blooming rose. Put #30 wire through styrene ball (see p. 58 Instructions: Bourbon Rose). Add ½ length #26 wire and bind wires at base of ball.

11. Begin gluing petals. Glue five Petal-c pieces on styrene ball and cover top of ball completely.

12. Layer two Petal-d pieces (mixing Pure silk habutai #8 and pure silk satin crepe #10), shift widthwise, and glue together. Make five sets. Glue each set around petals from step 11. For remaining ten Petal-d pieces, fold edge of petal over with your fingers. Then, glue one petal at a time.

13. Glue ten Petal-e pure silk crepe de Chine #10 pieces, while slightly lowering position of each petal. The young blooming rose is complete.

14. For each flower, add two #28 wires cut in half. Bind stem cloth at top. Make rosehip (see p. 51 Instructions: Ramanas Rose).

15. Make leaves. Sandwich #28 wire, cut in half, between a pair of leaf pieces and glue together. Shape veins using Ultra-thin Single Groove brass tip. Combine Leaf-A and -B to make three leaf stem (see p. 51, 52 Instructions: Ramanas Rose). Attach Stipule-D on back side of stem. Bundle three ½ length #28 wires and bind with stem cloth for about 25 mm / 1". This makes a flowerless stem.

16. Begin wrapping stem cloth below rosehip on young bloom. Combine Leaf-C and flowerless stem from step 15. Further bind stem cloths down, and then combine bloomed rose with three leaf stem. Attach Stipule-E to flower stem.

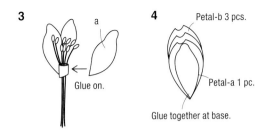

3

a

Glue on.

4

Petal-b 3 pcs.

Petal-a 1 pc.

Glue together at base.

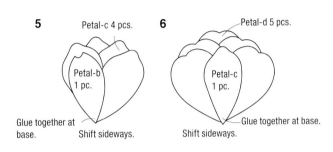

5

Petal-c 4 pcs.

Petal-b 1 pc.

Glue together at base.

Shift sideways.

6

Petal-d 5 pcs.

Petal-c 1 pc.

Glue together at base.

Shift sideways.

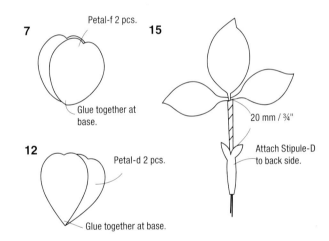

7

Petal-f 2 pcs.

Glue together at base.

15

20 mm / ¾"

Attach Stipule-D to back side.

12

Petal-d 2 pcs.

Glue together at base.

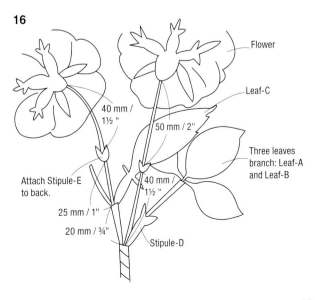

16

Flower

Leaf-C

Three leaves branch: Leaf-A and Leaf-B

40 mm / 1½ "

50 mm / 2"

40 mm / 1½ "

Attach Stipule-E to back.

25 mm / 1"

20 mm / ¾"

Stipule-D

Lady Rose

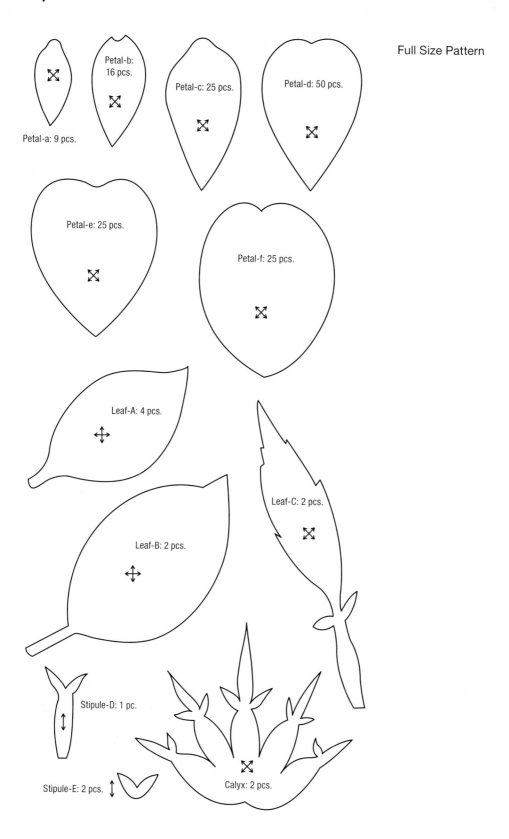

Full Size Pattern

Petal-a: 9 pcs.

Petal-b: 16 pcs.

Petal-c: 25 pcs.

Petal-d: 50 pcs.

Petal-e: 25 pcs.

Petal-f: 25 pcs.

Leaf-A: 4 pcs.

Leaf-B: 2 pcs.

Leaf-C: 2 pcs.

Stipule-D: 1 pc.

Stipule-E: 2 pcs.

Calyx: 2 pcs.

Full Size

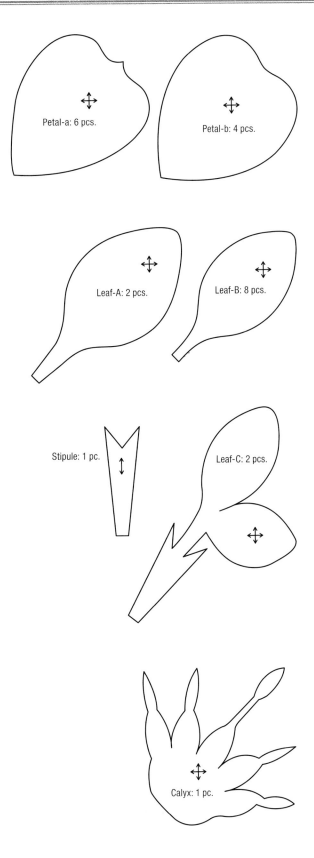

Petal-a: 6 pcs.

Petal-b: 4 pcs.

Leaf-A: 2 pcs.

Leaf-B: 8 pcs.

Stipule: 1 pc.

Leaf-C: 2 pcs.

Calyx: 1 pc.

p. 60 French Rose

Materials

Stiffened cloth
Pure silk habutai #8: Petal-a 30 pcs.
Pure silk habutai #10: Petal-b 10 pcs.
Pure silk georgette #6: Petal-b 8 pcs.
Pure silk crepe de Chine #10: Petal-b 7 pcs., Petal-c 15 pcs.
Pure silk crepe de Chine #14: Petal-d 5 pcs.
Cotton lawn: Leaf-A 2 pc., Leaf-B 4 pcs., Calyx 1 pc.
Thin silk (*Usukinu*): Stem cloth

Pips
Small mimosa pip 1 pc. After dyeing, cut stem in half.
Ultra-small rose pips: First dye pip heads. Then, glue together bundle of five pips and cut stem to 15 mm / ⅝". Make three sets.

Jimaki wires
½ length green #26 2pcs., ½ length #28 5 pcs.

Cotton

Brooch pin
25 mm / 1" wide 1 pc.

Brass soldering tip types
Ultra-thin Single Groove, 9 mm / ⅜"
Hemisphere, 15 mm / ⅝" Hemisphere

Sponge
Use soft sponge for all petals.

Dyeing

Rose (Pink + Scarlet + Sepia + Brown)
Olive Brown (Brown + Olive Green)
Leaf Green (Olive Green + Green + Sepia)

Petals: Uniformly dye very pale Olive Brown. While cloth is still damp, uniformly dye Petal-a cloths Rose. Dye Petal-b, -c, and -d pieces Rose to gradate. Drop pale Leaf Green at center and gradate softly. Dye outer, larger petal pieces pale Rose so that the outer petals are more pale.
Leaf, Calyx: Uniformly dye Leaf Green. Add Olive Brown on base of leaf while cloth is damp.
Stem cloth: Uniformly dye piece of thin silk Leaf Green. Cut thin silk into 5 mm / ¼" wide strips (see p. 80).
Pip: Dye mimosa pips light green and rose pips yellow.

Petal-a, -b, -c, -d

Pip

Stem

Leaf-B

Leaf-A

Calyx

Leaf-B

Rosehip

Brooch pin

Hot-press Diagram

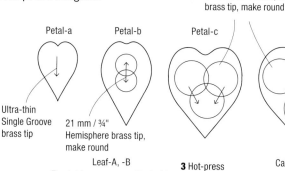

21 mm / ¾" Hemisphere brass tip, make round

Petal-a

Petal-b

Petal-c

Petal-d

Ultra-thin Single Groove brass tip

21 mm / ¾" Hemisphere brass tip, make round

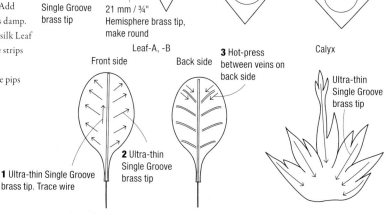

Leaf-A, -B

Front side

Back side

3 Hot-press between veins on back side

Calyx

1 Ultra-thin Single Groove brass tip. Trace wire

2 Ultra-thin Single Groove brass tip

Ultra-thin Single Groove brass tip

Steps

1. Make flower core. Glue mimosa pip with stem, that was cut in half, on the ½ length #26 wire. Glue on three bundles of rose pips so they encase mimosa pip. Bind stem cloth at base of pips.

2. Begin gluing on petals that are shaped according to the diagram. Glue six Petal-a pieces on, one at a time, around pip group.

3. Layer three Petal-a pieces, shift lengthwise, and glue together at base. Make eight sets. Glue each set on stem around petals from step 2.

4. Layer three Petal-b cloths, shift widthwise, and glue together at base. Make seven sets. Glue each set on stem around petals from step 3. Glue remaining four Petal-b pieces on, one at a time, while checking overall balance.

5. From the fifteen Petal-c pieces choose five or six and fold edge over with your fingers. Layer two Petal-b pieces, shift widthwise, and glue together at base. Make seven sets. Glue each set on stem around petals from step 4. Add remaining Petal-b cloth.

6. Fold edge of Petal-d pieces over with your fingers. Glue them on so that the five Petal-d pieces encircle petals from step 5.

7. Add three ½ length #28 wires to stem and bind top with stem cloth. Make rosehip (see p. 51, Instructions: Ramanas Rose).

8. Make leaves (see p. 51, Instructions: Ramanas Rose). Insert #26 wire, lengthwise, between a pair of Leaf-A pieces. Do same with #28 wire and a pair of Leaf-B pieces. Glue together and then shape leaves.

9. Begin to bind stem cloth under rosehip and combine leaves halfway down stem.

10. Attach brooch pin under flower base.

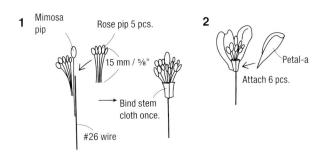

1. Mimosa pip · Rose pip 5 pcs. · 15 mm / ⅝" · Bind stem cloth once · #26 wire

2. Petal-a · Attach 6 pcs.

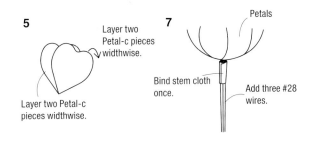

3. Layer three Petal-a pieces, shift lengthwise, and glue them together at base.

4. Petal-b 3 pcs. Layer widthwise and glue at base.

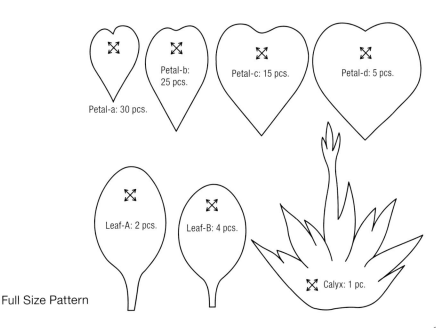

5. Layer two Petal-c pieces widthwise. · Layer two Petal-c pieces widthwise.

7. Petals · Bind stem cloth once. · Add three #28 wires.

Full Size Pattern

Petal-a: 30 pcs.

Petal-b: 25 pcs.

Petal-c: 15 pcs.

Petal-d: 5 pcs.

Leaf-A: 2 pcs.

Leaf-B: 4 pcs.

Calyx: 1 pc.

p. 70　Lily of the Valley

Materials

Stiffened cloth

Cotton lawn: Corolla 11 pcs. (Need two pieces that are 200 mm x 200 mm / 7⅞" x 7⅞" square)

B/B crepe de Chine or Pure silk crepe de Chine #14: Leaf-A 4 pcs.

Thin silk (*Usukinu*): Leaf-B 4 or 5 pcs. Stem clot

Pips

Medium or small plain ball pip 1 pc.

Rose pip with thread stem 10 pcs.

Jimaki wires

33 mm / 1¼" long green #22 1 pc., ½ length #28 2 pcs.

½ length white #28 1 pc.

Brooch pin

30 cm / 11¾" wide 1 pc.

Brass soldering tip types

Ultra-thin Single Groove, Small Lily of the Valley, Large Lily of the Valley, Line

Dyeing

Beige (Brown + Sepia)

Leaf Green (Olive Green + Green + Brown + Sepia)

Corolla: Uniformly dye very pale Beige, trace pattern, and cut out.

Leaf-A: Dye in pairs. Uniformly dye pale Beige. While cloth is still damp, add Leaf Green, from tip, and gradate base. Also, gradate Beige from base.

Leaf-B: Uniformly dye Beige. Trace pattern and cut out.

Stem cloth: Prepare one that is dyed Leaf Green and one that is dyed pale Leaf Green. Cut thin silk into 5 mm / ¼" wide strips (see p. 80).

Plain ball pip: Dye very pale Beige.

Rose pip: Trim off one pip head. Dye pip head yellow.

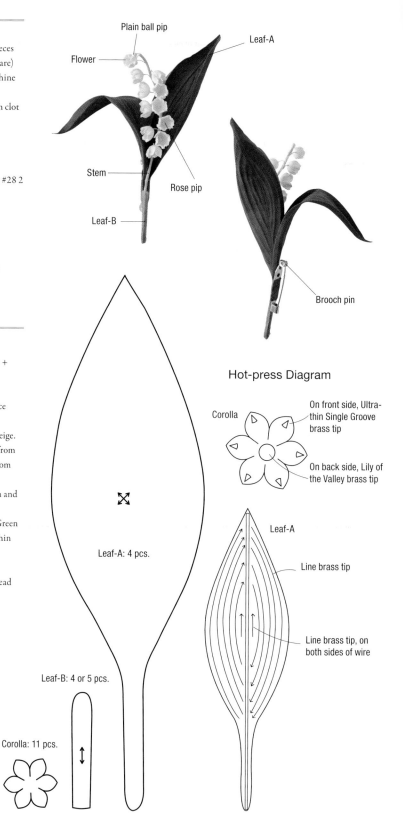

Plain ball pip

Leaf-A

Flower

Stem

Rose pip

Leaf-B

Brooch pin

Leaf-A: 4 pcs.

Leaf-B: 4 or 5 pcs.

Corolla: 11 pcs.

Full Size Pattern

Hot-press Diagram

Corolla

On front side, Ultra-thin Single Groove brass tip

On back side, Lily of the Valley brass tip

Leaf-A

Line brass tip

Line brass tip, on both sides of wire

Steps

1. Glue two pieces of dyed cloth together. Copy corolla pattern on cloth and cut out eleven corolla pieces.
2. Forcefully press down Ultra-thin Single Groove brass tip on edge of six corolla petals. Iron eight out of eleven corolla pieces (do not iron the other three).
3. Pierce hole at center of all eleven corolla pieces with an awl. On a soft sponge, push Lily of the Valley brass tip down at center to make round. Use Large Lily of the Valley brass tip on eight corolla pieces shaped in step 2. Use Small Lily of the Valley brass tip for the other three. Adjust shape while still warm. Re-open hole if plugged.
4. If the corolla cloth doesn't hold its shape after hot-pressing, add a small amount of glue by inserting a sharp needle between the petals. Then, try to reshape.
5. Apply glue on rose pip stem and insert stem into corolla cloth.
6. Halve stem on plain ball pip and bundle two plain ball pip heads at different heights. Add ½ length #28 white wire and bind with pale leaf green stem cloth. Begin with three corolla pieces, shaped using only Small Lily of the Valley brass tip, and attach them on the stem, alternating sides as shown in the figure. Curl flower stem using a bamboo skewer or an awl to tilt flower down.
7. Insert a ½ length #28 green wire between a pair of Leaf-A pieces that were dyed as a pair. Glue them together. Trim off excess wire.
8. Emboss veins using Line brass tip.
9. Wrap 30 mm / 1¼" long #22 wire with stem from Leaf-A piece. Face one Leaf-A piece towards the one with the wrapped wire. Then, wrap stem of Leaf-A piece with the other Leaf-A piece. Twist second Leaf-A in same direction as the first.
10. Attach brooch pin (closure is 15 mm / ⅝" above stem end) at back side of Leaf-A stem with stem cloth.
11. Combine flower and Leaf-A (trim off flower stem to match Leaf-A stem) and bind them with leaf green stem cloth. Cover stem end with stem cloth and bind below brooch pin again.
12. Attach four to five Leaf-B pieces around stem.

2

Push down.

Ultra-thin Single Groove brass tip

3

Large Lily of the Valley brass tip

4

Glue.

6

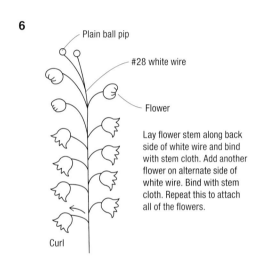

Plain ball pip

#28 white wire

Flower

Curl

Lay flower stem along back side of white wire and bind with stem cloth. Add another flower on alternate side of white wire. Bind with stem cloth. Repeat this to attach all of the flowers.

9

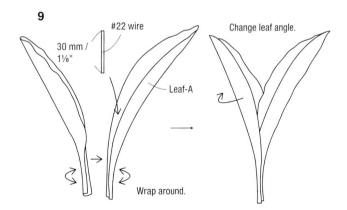

#22 wire

30 mm / 1⅛"

Leaf-A

Wrap around.

Change leaf angle.

p. 71 Snowdrop

Materials

Stiffened cloth

Pure silk satin crepe #10: Outer perianth 6 pcs.
Cotton lawn: Inner perianth 6 pcs.
Cotton satin: Leaf-A, Leaf-B 2 pcs. each
Pure silk Georgette #6: Spathe 1 pc.
Thin silk (*Usukinu*): Stem cloth, Ovary 3 or 4 pcs.,
Leaf-C 4 or 5 pcs.
Bulb 10 to 12 pcs., Roots

Pips

Ultra-small pointed pip 1 pc., Ultra-small rose pip 6 pcs.

Jimaki wires

⅔ length green #28 1 pc., ½ length green #28 2 pcs.
⅔ length white #33 2 pcs.

Styrene ball

16 mm / ⅝" wide rose core 1 pc.

Polymer clay
COPIC Sketch YG63
Brass soldering tip types

Small Petal, Single Groove Chrysanthemum, Ultra-thin Single Groove Chrysanthemum, Triple Groove Chrysanthemum

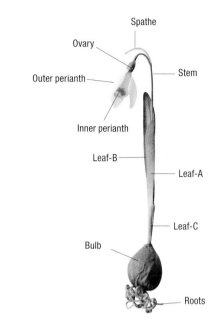

Dyeing

Leaf Green (Olive Green + Green + Brown + Sepia)
Beige (Sepia + Brown)
Dark Brown (Brown + Sepia + Green)

Outer perianth: Uniformly dye very pale Beige in pairs.

Inner perianth: Uniformly dye pale Beige in pairs. Gradate pale Leaf Green at base. Once completely dried, paint patterns on outside edge using Leaf Green.

Leaves: Dye in pairs. First, uniformly dye pale Beige. After excess moisture has evaporated, add Leaf Green from the tip of the leaf and gradate toward center. Once again, gradate Beige from base.

Stem cloth, Ovary: Uniformly dye piece of thin silk Leaf Green. Cut thin silk into 5 mm / ¼" wide strips (see p. 80). Ovary: Glue two pieces of thin silk together. Trace the ovary pattern on cloth and cut.

Leaf-C, Bulb: Uniformly dye piece of thin silk Beige. Fold thin silk in four layers. Trace pattern of Leaf-C and bulb on cloth and cut out required number of each component. Roots: Cut thin silk into 6 mm / ¼" wide strips.

Bulb: Fold piece of thin silk, dyed Dark Brown, into four layers. Trace pattern on cloth and cut out required number of bulb cloths.

Pips: Dye pointed pip Beige or pale green. Dye rose pips yellow.

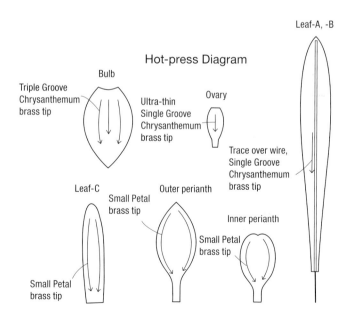

Hot-press Diagram

Steps

1. Glue pair of outer perianth pieces together using hard-type glue. Apply a very small amount of glue in dots. After glue has dried, shape with Small Petal brass tip.

2. Glue pair of inner perianth pieces together and shape with Small Petal brass tip.

3. For the leaves, insert ½ length #28 wire between a pair leaf pieces. Glue together. From leaf tip, trace wire with Single Groove Chrysanthemum brass tip to shape leaf. Wrap beige piece of thin silk around wire coming out of leaf bottom to make a root.

4. Glue ⅔ length #28 wire on pointed pip that had stem cut in half. Glue six rose pips, whose stem was cut to 8 mm / ¼", around the pointed pip. Bind with stem cloth.

5. Apply glue to base of inner perianth cloth and attach three pieces at equal intervals around stem from step 4. Glue outer perianth pieces between inner perianth pieces.

6. Make ovary using polymer clay. Shape ovary cloth using Ultra-thin Single Groove Chrysanthemum brass tip. Once polymer clay has solidified, glue ovary cloth to polymer clay.

7. Make the bulb. Cover styrene ball with polymer clay in the shape of a bulb. Make the bottom plump. Let clay harden.

8. Make spathe. Color two ⅔ length #33 white wires using COPIC Sketch marker. As shown in the figure, attach one wire on each side and twist to arch.

9. Start binding stem cloth from base of ovary. After binding about 15–20 mm / ⅝"–¾", combine spathe from step 8 and bind stem cloth about 90 mm / 3½" down from there. Then, cut stem cloth. Tilt flower down. Wrap beige thin silk on the three wires sticking out from bottom of stem to make roots.

10. Apply glue on base of Leaf-A piece and attach to front side of stem from step 9. Apply glue on base of Leaf-B piece and attach to back side of stem.

11. Shape Leaf-C pieces using Small Petal brass tip. Glue four or five Leaf-C pieces around base of leaves.

12. Shape bulb pieces using Triple Groove Chrysanthemum brass tip.

13. Punch hole in bulb from step 7 and insert in flower stem from step 10. Put glue in the bulb hole to prevent flower stem from falling off.

14. Glue five or six beige bulb pieces around the bulb. Then, glue five or six dark brown bulb pieces over that.

15. Curl roots sticking out from bulb by wrapping each root around an awl.

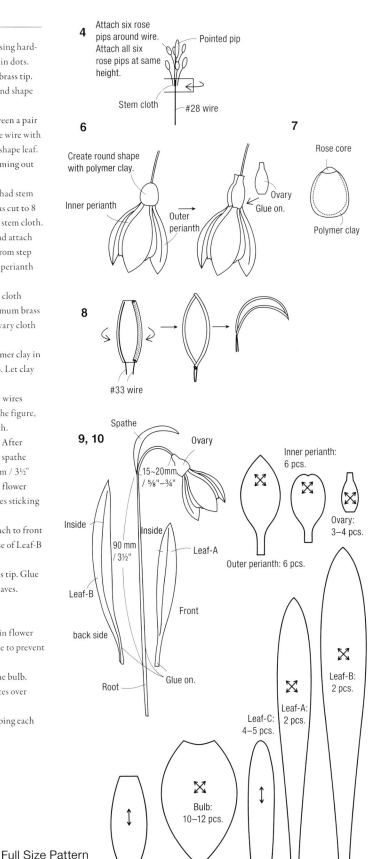

4 Attach six rose pips around wire. Attach all six rose pips at same height. — Pointed pip
Stem cloth — #28 wire

6 Create round shape with polymer clay. Inner perianth — Outer perianth

7 Rose core — Ovary Glue on. — Polymer clay

8 #33 wire

9, 10 Spathe — Ovary — 15~20mm / ⅝"–¾" — Inside — 90 mm / 3½" — Inside — Leaf-A — Leaf-B — back side — Front — Root — Glue on.

Inner perianth: 6 pcs.

Outer perianth: 6 pcs.

Ovary: 3–4 pcs.

Leaf-B: 2 pcs.

Leaf-A: 2 pcs.

Leaf-C: 4–5 pcs.

Bulb: 10–12 pcs.

Full Size Pattern

Spathe: 1 pc.

101

p. 72 Muscari

Materials

Stiffened cloth

Pure silk satin crepe #14: Flower 10 x 240 mm /
⅜" x 9½", 12 x 240 mm / ½" x 9½"

Poplin: Leaf-A, -B, -C 4 pcs. each, Stem cloth 10
x 100 mm / ⅜" x 4"

Thin silk (*Usukinu*): Wire cloth, Bulbs 8 to 10
pcs., Roots

Pips

Ultra-small plain ball pip 12 pcs., Small plain ball
pip 11 pcs., Medium plain ball pip 19 pcs.

Jimaki wires

½ length green #26 1 pc., ½ length #28 3 pcs., ½
length #30 6 pcs.

Styrene ball

20 mm / ¾" wide, egg-shape, 1 pc.

Polymer clay

Brass soldering tip types

Ultra-thin Single Groove Chrysanthemum,
Triple Groove Chrysanthemum

Dyeing

Light Blue (Turquoise Blue + Blue + Brown)
Leaf Green (Olive Green + Green + Brown +
Sepia)
Beige (Sepia + Brown)
Dark Brown (Brown + Sepia + Green)

Flower: Uniformly dye flower pale Light Blue.
Leaf-A, -B, -C: Uniformly dye pale Beige in pairs.
Gradate pale Leaf Dye in pairs. First, uniformly
dye pale Beige. After excess moisture has
evaporated, add Leaf Green from the tip of the
leaf and gradate to center. Once again, gradate
Beige from the base.
Stem cloth: Uniformly dye a piece of thin silk
Leaf Green.
Bulbs: Uniformly dye piece of thin silk Beige.
Fold in four layers, trace pattern, and cut out.
After bulb pieces are cut out, gradate Dark
Brown at top and bottom.
Wire cloth: Uniformly dye a piece of thin silk
Leaf Green. Cut into 4 mm / ⅛" wide strips and 6
mm / ¼" wide strips (see p. 80).
Roots: Uniformly dye a piece of thin silk Beige.
Cut into 5 mm / ¼" wide strips (see p. 80).
Pips: Dye pale green color.

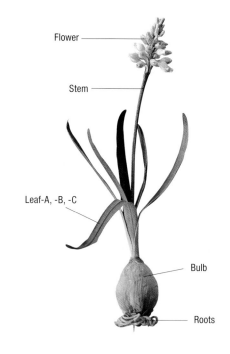

Flower
Stem
Leaf-A, -B, -C
Bulb
Roots

Hot-press Diagram

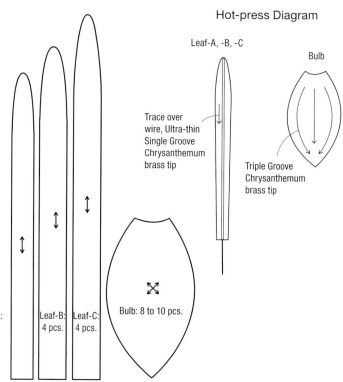

Leaf-A, -B, -C

Trace over
wire, Ultra-thin
Single Groove
Chrysanthemum
brass tip

Bulb

Triple Groove
Chrysanthemum
brass tip

Leaf-A:
4 pcs.

Leaf-B:
4 pcs.

Leaf-C:
4 pcs.

Bulb: 8 to 10 pcs.

Full Size Pattern

Steps

1. Make flowers. Pierce a hole at center of a cloth that was cut to 10 x 8 mm / ⅜" x ¼" with an awl. Thread an ultra-small, plain ball pip through hole. Apply glue and wrap pip head with cloth. Once glue has dried, cut off tip and open cut edge by piercing with an awl. Make twelve sets.

2. Thread small plain ball pip through flower cloth, cut and assemble in the same manner as step 1 with 10 x 10 mm / ¼" x ¼" pieces. Make eleven sets.

3. Thread medium, plain ball pip through the flower cloth, cut and assemble with 12 x 12 mm / ½" x ½" pieces in the same manner as step 1. Make nineteen sets.

4. Attach three cloth covered ultra-small pips from step 1 around a ½ length #26 wire and bind with 4 mm / ⅛" wide stem cloth. Trim off pip stems where they stick out from the stem cloth.

5. For the second row, attach four cloth covered, ultra-small pips from step 1 without overlapping the first row. Bind stem cloth. Trim off pip stems. From third row onward, combine cloth covered pips to make flower.

6. For small to medium pips, leave stem longer when covering pip head with a piece of thin silk. Combine third row: five ultra-small pips, forth row: five small pips, fifth row: six small pips, sixth row: six medium pips, seventh/eighth row: four medium pips, ninth row: five medium pips.

7. Add three ½ length #28 wires to the flower stem and bind with 6 mm / ¼" wide wire cloth for 90–100 mm / 3½"–4". Then, wrap with stem cloth lengthwise.

8. Make the leaves. Sandwich a ½ length #30 wire between a pair of leaf pieces and glue. Press Ultra-thin Single Groove Chrysanthemum brass tip over the wire, from tip of leaf.

9. Wrap a piece of beige thin silk separately on each wire, extending from flower stem and wire on leaf pieces. This will become the roots. Glue base of each leaf piece on flower stem so that leaves encase flower stem.

10. Make the bulb. Cover styrene ball with polymer clay. Let clay harden.

11. Shape bulb cloths using Triple Groove Chrysanthemum brass tip.

12. Punch a hole in bulb from step 10 and add flower stem from step 9. Apply glue to flower stem where it's hidden inside the bulb to prevent bulb from coming off.

13. Glue eight to ten pieces of bulb cloth from step 11 around the bulb.

14. Wrap roots that extend from the bulb around an awl to curl them.

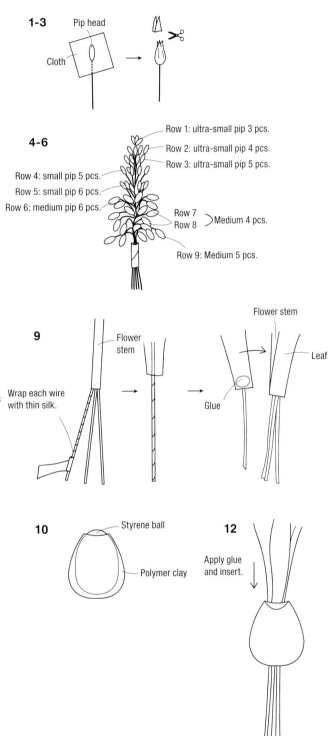

1-3

Pip head

Cloth

4-6

Row 1: ultra-small pip 3 pcs.
Row 2: ultra-small pip 4 pcs.
Row 3: ultra-small pip 5 pcs.

Row 4: small pip 5 pcs.
Row 5: small pip 6 pcs.
Row 6: medium pip 6 pcs.

Row 7
Row 8 } Medium 4 pcs.

Row 9: Medium 5 pcs.

9

Flower stem

Wrap each wire with thin silk.

Flower stem

Leaf

Glue

10

Styrene ball

Polymer clay

12

Apply glue and insert.

p. 73 **Narcissus**

Materials

Stiffened cloth

Pure silk satin crepe #10: Outer perianth 6 pcs.,
Inner perianth 6 pc.

Pure silk satin crepe #14: Corona 1 pc.

Cotton satin: Leaf-A, -B, -C, -D 2 pcs. each

Poplin: Stem cloth 10 x 130 mm / ⅜" x 5⅛"

Pure silk Georgette #6: Spathe 1 pc.

Thin silk (*Usukinu*): Stem cloth, Wire cloth,
Bulb 10 to 12 pcs.

Leaf-E 25 x 50 mm / 1" x 2", Roots

Pips

Ultra-small pip 3 half-length pcs.

Ultra-small rose pip 6 half-length pcs.

Jimaki wires

½ length green #26 1 pc., ⅔ length #28 4 pcs.

½ length white #33 6 pcs.

Styrene ball

Styrene ball - 30 mm / 1¾" diameter 1 pc.

Polymer clay

Brass soldering tip types

Ultra-thin Single Groove, Ultra-thin Petal,
Small Petal, Medium Petal, Triple Groove
Chrysanthemum

Dyeing

Yellow Brown (Yellow + Sepia + Olive Green)

Leaf Green (Olive Green + Green + Sepia)

Dark Brown (Brown + Sepia + a small amount of
Leaf Green)

Beige (Sepia + a small amount of Dark Brown)

Outer and Inner perianth: Dye in pairs with
Yellow Brown diluted with twice as much water.
Gradate Leaf Green at base.

Corona: Dye Yellow Brown and gradate Beige
at base.

Leaf-A, -B, -C, -D: After uniformly dyeing in
Beige, gradate Leaf Green from the tip.

Stem cloth: Uniformly dye Leaf Green.

Spathe: After dyeing uniformly Beige, gradate
Leaf Green at base.

Leaf-E: Uniformly dye very pale Beige.

Stem cloth, wire cloth: Uniformly dye a piece of
thin silk Leaf Green. Cut thin silk into 5 mm /
¼" wide strips (see p. 80).

Bulbs, Roots: Uniformly dye a piece of thin
silk Beige. Fold thin silk into four layers. Trace
pattern on cloth and cut out required number of
bulb cloths. Cut thin silk into 6 mm / ¼" wide
strips.

Bulbs: Uniformly dye a piece of thin silk Dark
Brown. Fold into four layers. Trace pattern on
cloth and cut out five to six bulbs.

Pips: Dye yellow.

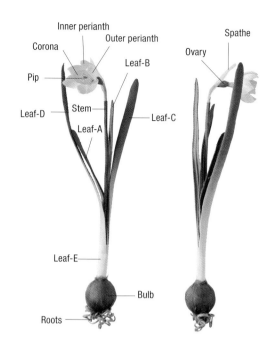

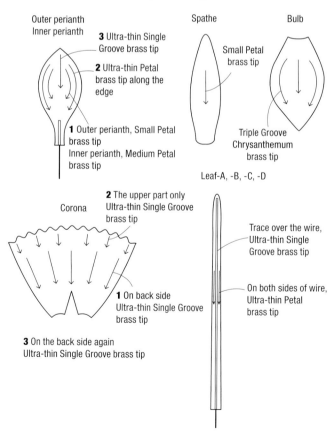

Hot-press Diagram

Outer perianth
Inner perianth

3 Ultra-thin Single
Groove brass tip

2 Ultra-thin Petal
brass tip along the
edge

1 Outer perianth, Small Petal
brass tip
Inner perianth, Medium Petal
brass tip

Spathe

Small Petal
brass tip

Bulb

Triple Groove
Chrysanthemum
brass tip

Leaf-A, -B, -C, -D

Corona

2 The upper part only
Ultra-thin Single Groove
brass tip

1 On back side
Ultra-thin Single Groove
brass tip

3 On the back side again
Ultra-thin Single Groove brass tip

Trace over the wire,
Ultra-thin Single
Groove brass tip

On both sides of wire,
Ultra-thin Petal
brass tip

Steps

1. For both outer and inner perianth, insert a ½ length #33 white wire between two pieces of cloth and glue together. Then, shape perianth pieces according to the diagram.
2. Shape corona cloth according to diagram.
3. Cut #26 wire in half. Then, glue three ultra-small plain ball pips around the ½ length #26 wire.
4. 10 mm / ⅜" below pip heads, bind a thin silk strip once. Then, glue six ultra-small rose pips around the plain ball pips.
5. Bind a thin silk strip over the thin silk strip bound in step 4 for about 15 mm / ⅝".
6. Make ovary using polymer clay. See figure 6.
7. Once clay has hardened, glue edges of corona to make a circular shape. Attach to top of ovary.
8. Attach three inner perianths, evenly spaced around corona. Then, attach outer perianth to fill the gap.
9. Cover base of flower with a thin silk strip as well as the ovary. Continue to bind for another 15 mm / ⅝".
10. Attach spathe cloth, which has been hot-pressed using Small Petal brass tip on wire from step 9, so that the spathe gently wraps around it.
11. Fold stem cloth in half lengthwise. As shown in figure 11, glue stem cloth so it covers wire. Trim off both edges of stem cloth. Trim off excess wire while leaving 20 mm / ¾" from end of stem cloth.
12. Make Leaf-A, -B, -C, -D. Sandwich ⅔ length #28 wire with a pair of leaf cloths and glue together. Shape each leaf piece using a soldering iron. Bind thin silk, for roots, on wire of each leaf piece.
13. Attach leaf pieces on flower stem from step 11.
14. Wrap two or three Leaf-E pieces around base of leaves.
15. Pierce a hole in the styrene ball with an awl and insert flower from step 14. Put glue in bulb hole to keep the flower from coming off.
16. Cover styrene ball with bulb pieces that are shaped according to the diagram. First, glue on five or six beige bulb pieces and then glue five or six dark brown bulb cloths over those.
17. Wrap roots that extend from the bulb around an awl to curl them.

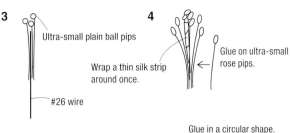

3
Ultra-small plain ball pips
#26 wire

4
Glue on ultra-small rose pips.
Wrap a thin silk strip around once.

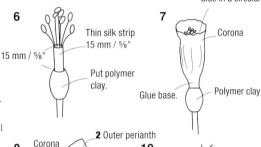

6
Thin silk strip 15 mm / ⅝"
15 mm / ⅝"
Put polymer clay.

7
Glue in a circular shape.
Corona
Glue base.
Polymer clay

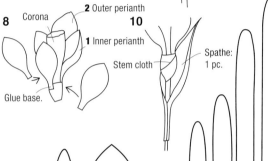

8
Corona
2 Outer perianth
1 Inner perianth
Glue base.

10
Spathe: 1 pc.
Stem cloth

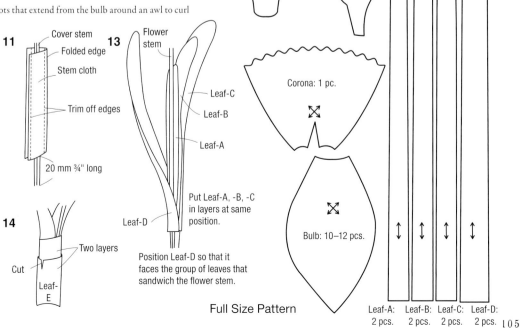

11
Cover stem
Folded edge
Stem cloth
Trim off edges
20 mm ¾" long

13
Flower stem
Leaf-C
Leaf-B
Leaf-A
Leaf-D
Put Leaf-A, -B, -C in layers at same position.
Position Leaf-D so that it faces the group of leaves that sandwich the flower stem.

14
Two layers
Cut
Leaf-E

Spathe: 1 pc.

Outer perianth: 6 pcs.

Inner perianth: 6 pcs.

Corona: 1 pc.

Bulb: 10–12 pcs.

Leaf-A: 2 pcs.   Leaf-B: 2 pcs.   Leaf-C: 2 pcs.   Leaf-D: 2 pcs.

Full Size Pattern

p. 6　Pattern: Frilly Pansy

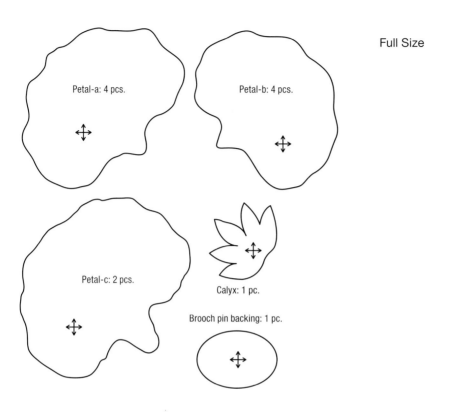

Full Size

Petal-a: 4 pcs.

Petal-b: 4 pcs.

Petal-c: 2 pcs.

Calyx: 1 pc.

Brooch pin backing: 1 pc.

p. 26　Pattern: Poppy Anemone

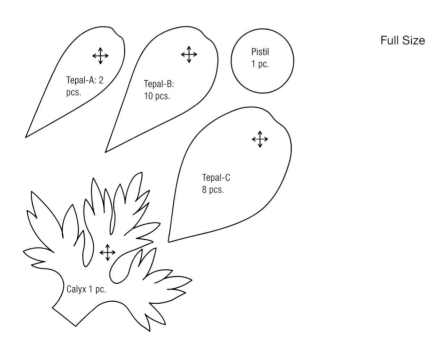

Full Size

Tepal-A: 2 pcs.

Tepal-B: 10 pcs.

Pistil 1 pc.

Tepal-C 8 pcs.

Calyx 1 pc.

p. 10   Pattern: French Hydrangea

Full Size

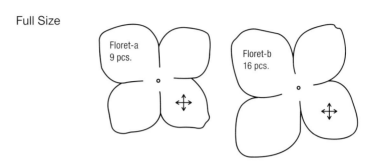

Floret-a
9 pcs.

Floret-b
16 pcs.

p. 30   Pattern: Christmas Rose

Full Size

Tepal-A 6 pcs.

Tepal-B 4 pcs.

Nectary 2 pcs.

Bud 1 pc.

Bract-B 4 pcs.

Bract-A 4 pcs.

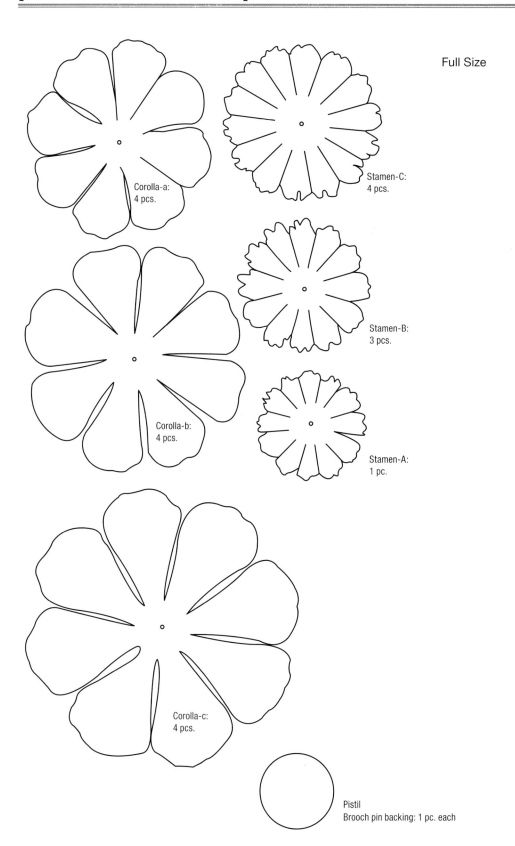

Full Size

Corolla-a:
4 pcs.

Stamen-C:
4 pcs.

Corolla-b:
4 pcs.

Stamen-B:
3 pcs.

Stamen-A:
1 pc.

Corolla-c:
4 pcs.

Pistil
Brooch pin backing: 1 pc. each

Full Size

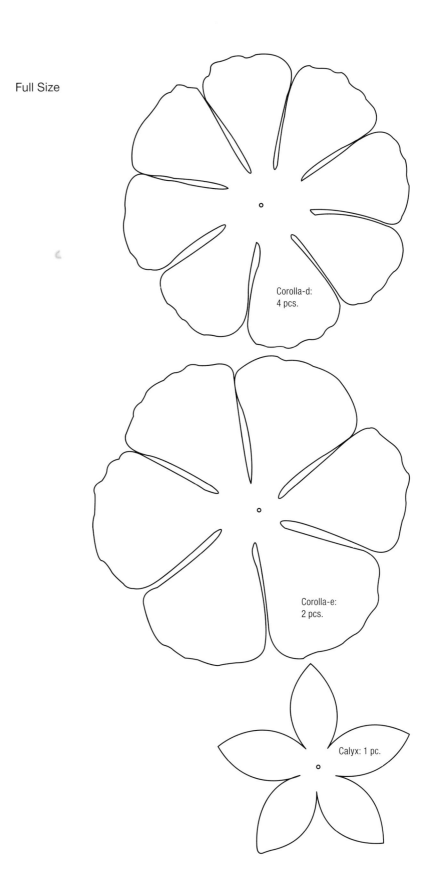

Corolla-d:
4 pcs.

Corolla-e:
2 pcs.

Calyx: 1 pc.

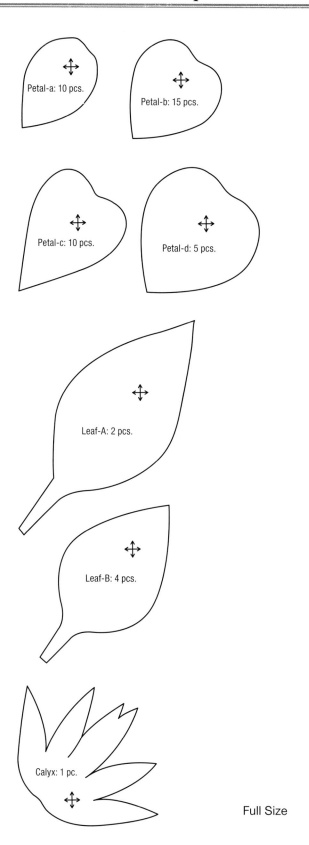

Petal-a: 10 pcs.

Petal-b: 15 pcs.

Petal-c: 10 pcs.

Petal-d: 5 pcs.

Leaf-A: 2 pcs.

Leaf-B: 4 pcs.

Calyx: 1 pc.

Full Size

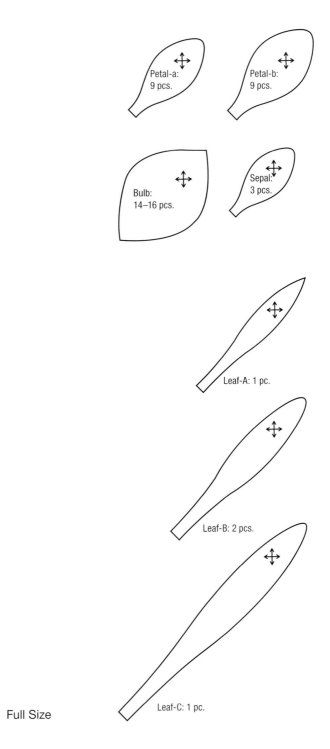

Petal-a:
9 pcs.

Petal-b:
9 pcs.

Bulb:
14–16 pcs.

Sepal:
3 pcs.

Leaf-A: 1 pc.

Leaf-B: 2 pcs.

Leaf-C: 1 pc.

Full Size

About the Author

Utopiano's botanical fabric art is widely exhibited. She ranges far and wide in nature to understand and translate it with her work. She observes plants, collected directly from the field, and makes patterns to then create fabric flowers. She doesn't just replicate the plant but aims to represent everything about it—including invisible elements like scent, texture, power, and presence. Several times a year, in addition to her solo exhibitions, utopiano holds collaborative exhibitions with artists who work with different materials. She offers in-person and online lessons at her atelier.

http://utopiano.tumblr.com

Other Schiffer Books on Related Subjects:

Blooming Paper: How to Handcraft Paper Flowers and Botanicals, Laura Reed, ISBN 978-0-7643-6208-8

Forever Flowers: Dry, Preserve, Display, Antonia De Vere, ISBN 978-0-7643-6207-1

The Intentional Thread: A Guide to Drawing, Gesture, and Color in Stitch, Susan Brandeis, ISBN 978-0-7643-5743-5

English edition copyright © 2022 by Schiffer Publishing, Ltd.

Library of Congress Control Number: 2022941118

ISBN: 978-0-7643-6421-1

Printed in India

Published by Schiffer Publishing, Ltd.
4880 Lower Valley Road
Atglen, PA 19310
Phone: (610) 593-1777; Fax: (610) 593-2002
Email: Info@schifferbooks.com
Web: www.schifferbooks.com

For our complete selection of fine books on this and related subjects, please visit our website at www.schifferbooks.com. You may also write for a free catalog.

Schiffer Publishing's titles are available at special discounts for bulk purchases for sales promotions or premiums. Special editions, including personalized covers, corporate imprints, and excerpts, can be created in large quantities for special needs. For more information, contact the publisher.

We are always looking for people to write books on new and related subjects. If you have an idea for a book, please contact us at proposals@schifferbooks.com.

Originally published as *Nunohana Hyohon*
© 2017 utopiano
© 2017 GRAPHIC-SHA PUBLISHING CO., LTD
First designed and published in Japan in 2017 by Graphic-sha Publishing Co. Ltd.
English edition published in the United States of America in 2022 by Schiffer Publishing, Ltd.
English translation rights arranged with Graphic-sha Publishing Co, Ltd. through Japan UNI Agency, Inc., Tokyo

Original edition creative staff

Photos:	Kiyoko Eto, utopiano (pgs. 2, 38, 39, 42, 43, 46, 47, 54, 55, 62, 63)
Book design:	Motoko Kitsukawa
Drawing:	Miyuki Oshima
Editing:	Ayako Enaka (Graphic-sha Publishing)
Material Cooperation:	Sansei Inc.
Photo shooting cooperation:	Five from the Ground, Antique Mise
Special cooperation:	Kyoko Fujii (KoubutuAsobi), Eita Kitayama, Patrone

English edition creative staff

English translation:	Kevin Wilson
English edition layout:	Shinichi Ishioka
Foreign edition production and management:	Takako Motoki (Graphic-sha Publishing)